THE MECCANO APPRENTICE

JEFFREY ROY BYRNE

The Meccano Apprentice

Published by Jeffrey Roy Byrne
Publishing partner: Paragon Publishing, Rothersthorpe
First published 2017
© Jeffrey Roy Byrne 2017

ISBN 978-1-78222-533-1

Book design, layout and production management by Into Print
www.intoprint.net
+44 (0)1604 832149

Printed and bound in UK and USA by Lightning Source

Foreword

Of all my memories of Meccano one of the most vivid is the day I tried to rocket power a wheeled Dinky Toy base with a steel tube full of gunpowder. I told my friends about the great experiment and lit the fuse. The vehicle set off at a furious pace along the Toolroom floor until suddenly – and quite spectacularly – it blew up!

Fortunately no one was hurt but the factory was rocked to its very foundations and I came within a hair's breadth of going 'up the road.' The only thing that saved me from that ignoble exit was the fact that I was due to go for my National Service in the R A F in a few weeks time. Thereafter I was known to some as Werner Von Byrne, (a parody of Werner Von Braun the Nazi rocket expert of WW2), and to others as 'That bloody idiot who nearly blew us all up!'

Looking back I suppose I would be labelled a character, one of many in that sprawling factory which, for over fifty years, made so many of the worlds most sought after toys. During my engineering career I worked in many factories, each with its own special atmosphere, some happy, others downright depressing, but one thing was common to them all – it was just a job. Meccano however, was very different. To work in that unique factory was like being part of one huge family.

In some respects this feeling was perhaps typical of a business in the fifties where the founding family retained control – Frank Hornby's son, Roland, was still Meccano's President – but Meccano owed its special atmosphere more to the products which poured from the production lines: the legendary Dinky Toys, Hornby Trains and Meccano Construction Sets, and knowing we were part of something quite unique, we

Meccano-ites closed our ranks and revelled in our exalted status. But even then times were changing. The plastic revolution was already forging ahead and, flexing their silicon chip muscles, the electronic giants were waiting in the wings.

Ten years after starting my apprenticeship I drove away through the thousands of home-going Meccano workers for the last time. I took with me my toolbox, a ringing in my ears from my farewell Toolroom Rally and a coveted sheet of headed Company paper which informed the world that I was a time-served Meccano toolmaker.

I left behind many friends and equally as many well-intentioned promises to drop in sometime and see them all again. Somehow I never managed to keep those promises, and it was not until a Sunday afternoon in 1981 that I made a belated return to Frank Hornby's historic factory.

Outwardly the building still fitted my memory's blueprint, but when I crossed the deserted road and peered in through a small window set in one of the main doors, I looked upon unrecognisable chaos.

Most of the roof had gone, leaving old electric cables trailing forlornly down from the few remaining girders like the remnants of broken spiders' webs. Surrounded by oil-rainbowed puddles and debris, a bulldozer stood waiting to continue the destruction on Monday morning.

Although I knew, as most of the world knew, that those massive doors had long since closed forever behind the last redundant worker, I was still unprepared for the shock of this sad and total desolation.

For a long time I stood gazing, almost unseeing, through that tiny window as the decades rolled away and in their hundreds and in their thousands they came flooding back: the faces; the voices; the memories ...

Walking to the Future

It was a wide road; wide and long and ruler straight. At the top, near the cross-roads, a small sign fixed high on a red-brick shop wall informed the stranger that this was BINNS ROAD. At the bottom, and half a mile distant down that long, straight hill, where the road turned right, reared the massive bulk of Crawford's Biscuit Works.

For the first hundred yards or so the pavements were edged by rows of neat, terraced houses, but beyond the boundaries of Runic Street to the right and Sapphire Street on the left the curtained windows were replaced by dark factory walls. On the Runic Street side endless streams of overalls and tin ware flowed from the production lines but across the road, inside a sprawling brick building with mesh covered windows, the brightly coloured dreams of millions of small boys were being created.

And it was towards those smoke-stained walls that a small scrubbed and Brylcreemed figure came walking one grey autumn morning. Under his arm was a brown paper parcel containing sandwiches and a new overall coat, turned up at the bottom by his mother, and in his heart was trepidation for what awaited him in this alien world of industry.

Except for a few scattered figures he was alone. The hurrying, chattering workers who had thronged the road a short time before were gone now, busy with familiar tasks inside the warm, brightly lit factories, leaving the cold breeze free to play with the litter of their passing. Down the hill he came, the new apprentice, across the end of Sapphire Street, past the tiny corner shop and on into the long, dark shadow of his future.

A few minutes walk brought him to a wide cul-de-sac flanked by the high factory walls. On the right, a line of neatly parked cars, at the end the huge, closed doors of the main entrance, and above those doors, chiselled in stone, was the name which had weaved many of his own so recent childhood dreams: MECCANO.

For a few moments the small figure stood at the corner, lost in the loneliness of his fifteen short years. Then, tightening his grip on the parcel he walked towards the small, green door waiting at the end of the pavement.

The Start of it All

I pushed the door open. The room was high and tiny. To the left was a counter with glass panels above, looking into a large office busy with people. On a narrow bench opposite, a heavily made-up girl sat smoking a cigarette. To my nervous, virgin eyes she was beautiful.

The vision directed a bored plume of smoke at the ceiling. 'Lukin' fera job are yer?' she asked sociably.

'No! No!' I answered hurriedly, blushing to the roots of my Brylcreemed hair. 'I'm an apprentice toolmaker, I start work this morning.'

The vivid, scarlet lips smiled knowingly. 'A toolmaker are ya? Some of me frens werk 'ere so I know all about yous toolroom fellas.'

I was not destined to discover what she meant by that remark until much later. At that moment the glass panel slid back and a male voice asked coldly, 'And what can we do for you young man?'

A tall, dark haired man, eyebrows raised enquiringly, was framed at the window. I hastened to explain who I was. 'I'm the apprentice toolmaker. I was told to come at nine o'clock this morning.'

The eyebrows lowered. 'Ah yes, I know all about you. We'll just fill in a few forms and someone will come for you.'

A few minutes later I was an employee of Meccano Limited, Binns Road, Liverpool. I had a small book of company rules, my pay was twenty three shillings a week and my clock number was 629.

'Now just wait here,' said the man, 'and you'll be collected shortly.'

The window slid shut leaving me standing by the counter trying to think of something sensible to say to my exotic companion. She dropped her cigarette on the floor, ground it slowly under her foot and looked up. 'You're lucky you are,' she announced.

'Me? Why?' I could feel my face flaming.

'You've gorra job. I've been sittin' 'ere ferages waitin' to see someone. It's always the same wit us gerls, dey cudden care less – the bleeders!' Snapping her handbag open she took out a packet of Woodbines.

I fumbled for words. I'd never met such a forward, aggressive girl before and was totally out of my depth. A feeble response finally surfaced. 'Oh. I see. You're looking for a job then?'

Smoke plumed irritably upwards and the sharp reply abruptly ended the conversation. 'Well I'm not sittin' ere fer the good of me 'ealth am I yer silly bugger!'

The door at the other end of the room suddenly opened to reveal a small figure wearing a dirt-streaked work coat. He eyed the girl. 'You the new apprentice?'

Mascara'd eyes flashed. 'Bugger off short arse! I wudden be seen dead wit you!'

'I'm the apprentice,' I volunteered hastily.

He stood back, holding the door open. 'Come on then, I'll show you where to put your coat.'

'Bye.' I offered, stepping through a smoky, scented cloud into my new world.

'Tara,' and to my still grinning guide, 'and drop dead shrimp!'

'Scrubber!' he exclaimed, as the door closed behind us.

'This place is full of them.'

He held out his hand. 'I'm Andy.'

'Roy.'

We shook hands. He was about my height, sallow complexioned, with a wide, cheerful, mouth and hair carefully combed up into a large quiff. For a few moments he waited as I looked round curiously. We were standing in a high, wide area with the walls painted green to about shoulder height and cream above, this narrowed to a passage on the right. In the opposite wall was a small door with a bank of windows to the left which were suddenly illuminated by a flash of flame.

'That's the Hardening Shop,' my new friend informed me, inclining his head towards the windows, 'and that's the door to Sinbad's office.'

'Sinbad?'

He frowned. 'Jack Simpson, the Toolroom Foreman. He's alright I suppose, but we'd better move in case he comes out and catches us standing around, come on.' He walked briskly away to the left.

A nasty thought that, being caught standing around in my first few minutes as an employee. I hurried after him.

A little further on, at a junction, we came to a big, wooden box with windows in the sides set on tall, spindly legs. To one end was fitted a large, flat circular metal ring, pierced with hundreds of small holes, each one numbered by a small disc. From the centre radiated a long, steel bar with a narrow pointer at one end and through the glass-panelled sides a paper covered drum was visible, and it ticked with a slow, metallic malevolence. This was the guardian of the Company's time - The Clock; a machine which, together with its electronic successors, was to rule my coming and going at Meccano for the next ten years – to the minute!

Andy explained the working of this strange machine. 'What's your clock number?'

I'd forgotten already. 'Six something I think. Just a minute, I'll see if it's on this form.' I searched for the slip of paper. 'Got it – six two nine.'

He looked at the numbers on the ring, counting under his breath. 'Here it is, up here on the left,' he said, touching the hole. 'Now remember exactly where it is 'cos if you're nearly late in the morning you don't want to have to mess about looking for your number – you could lose a quarter of an hour's pay.'

'Why?' I asked, puzzled.

The explanation was complicated and by the time it was finished my meagre stock of confidence was just about down to zero.

'It's like this,' said Andy. 'You're allowed three minutes late, after that you lose fifteen minutes pay and if you're late so many times – I forget how many – you get a warning. If you still keep coming late you'll be suspended for a week with no pay. Okay?'

It wasn't okay but I nodded anyway.

He continued. 'You turn this arm until the pointer is in line with your number and press it into the hole, that stamps the time by your number on the paper inside. Clock on in the morning, at the end of dinner time and again at night when you knock off – and never clock someone else's number, even if they ask you to. If you get caught it's straight up the road! Okay?'

There was no nod this time, I was in a state of mild shock. 'What's up the road?'

'Dead sack! Out! Finished!' He swung the arm violently sending it spinning round and round. 'Bloody clock!' he said viciously. 'Can't stand the bloody thing!'

A sentiment I was rapidly beginning to echo.

We returned along the passage and continued into an area lined on both sides by large, framed boxes covered in wire mesh, like giant chicken runs, with coats hanging all round the inside. Andy opened one of the doors. 'This is the Toolroom's, hang your coat up – if you can find a hook.'

It was quiet in the cloakroom, the noise of machinery which had been steadily growing louder as we walked deeper into the factory was muffled almost to a whisper by the rows of damp-smelling clothing which surrounded me. Eventually I found a vacant hook and as I donned my fawn work-coat, feeling its stiff, creased newness, a feeling of panic over-whelmed me. Outside this quiet cocoon of empty coats lay the noisy, adult world of their unknown owners; a world I was being rushed into before I was ready. I couldn't do it! I'd have to go home!

Then Andy's voice came. 'Come on! Are you having a bloody bath in there! Sinbad will be wondering where the bloody hell we are!'

Almost without realising I replied. 'Okay I'm coming now.' And picking up the parcel of sandwiches, I walked away from my childhood.

'You took long enough,' commented Andy as I closed the door.

'Couldn't find a hook with all those coats,' I said. 'There must be a lot of people in the Toolroom.'

'About fifty I think,' he replied. 'Now let's get a move on.'

We came to a T junction with a wide corridor stretching away in both directions. The clatter of machines was louder, accompanied by a rhythmic thumping which could be felt through the floor. An oily, metallic smell hung in the air. As we turned right a man in overalls went through a small door in the opposite wall. 'That's the bog,' remarked Andy, 'but there's a better one at the end of the passage, I'll show you later.'

With a familiarity I envied, my guide gave names to the open doors and hatches as we passed. On the right the Maintenance Shop, the Tool Stores, Tool Repair and the Toolroom. On the other side a long line of windows bordered the vast, machinery filled Press Shop. Girls wearing green overalls and headscarves were sitting by the windows swinging the handles on some sort of small press. I eyed them curiously, until one looked round, staring back unsmiling; embarrassed, I hurriedly turned away.

The door to my apprenticeship was wide and green with windows in the upper half. Andy slid it open and we were in a huge, square room filled with the hum of electric motors and sharp, metallic noises. In front of me a wide passage paved with metal tiles and flanked on both sides by lines of grey machines, ended at a raised office with large, glass windows. Another passage, edged by fawn coated men working at benches, went off to the left until it turned right with yet more men and benches lined along the wall; and everywhere machines whined and clicked and hummed. It was fascinating.

'Don't stand there gawping! Sinbad can see us! Come on!' Andy's urgent voice brought me back to reality in a hurry. I followed along the passage towards those glinting office windows. That must be where the dreaded Sinbad lurked; was he even now watching me from behind that shining glass? I hoped not.

About half way along we stopped at two low machines fixed at right angles to the wall.

'Here we are,' said Andy. 'Come over by the wall, Sinbad

can't see us there.' He opened the door of a small, steel locker and looked at my parcel. 'Those your sarnies?"

'Yes.'

He opened the door. 'Stick 'em in here with mine.'

I pushed the parcel onto the shelf and closed the door.

Andy pointed to the machine. 'This is called a shaper. Ever seen one before?'

I shook my head. 'No.'

'Okay. Well what it does is to shape blocks of metal – that's why it's called a shaper. See the way Chris's machine is going. Hey Chris, this is the new lad – his name's Roy.'

The small apprentice with blond, curly hair working on the other shaper looked over his shoulder and raised a hand. 'Hiya.'

I raised my own hand. 'Hi.'

'Right,' said Andy. 'Now watch me.' He pressed a button on the side of the machine and the motor began to hum. 'Green for on.' He pressed the red button alongside with a flourish and the motor died, 'and red for off. You start it up.'

I jabbed the button and immediately the motor whined into life.

'Okay. Now this lever starts the machine.' He pulled a long lever on the side of the machine and the top part of the shaper began to slide smoothly backwards and forwards. 'That's called the ram, and on the front is the vice to hold the steel you're machining. Ever seen a vice before?'

'Yes,' I said. 'My dad's got one in the shed at home, I've used it many times.'

'Okay. Now this is the traverse.' He turned a small knob on a thin bar rocking in time to the ram and shavings began to fly off the block of metal held in the vice as it travelled slowly across the front of the machine. Andy pointed to a small piece of steel fixed in a holder on the front of the ram and which was cutting into the job. 'That's the toolbit. It's made out of hardened high-speed steel so it can cut into softer metal, okay?'

'Okay.'

'And when the toolbit gets blunt you have to take it out and grind a sharp edge on it again, I'll show you how to do that later – okay?'

'Okay,' I repeated, watching in fascination as the small chips of metal pinged against the steel guard.

'And another thing,' continued Andy. 'When you're working at the front like this don't forget that Sinbad can see you from his office so look busy even if you're not.'

I hurriedly to my hands out of my pockets and stood up straight.

A man walked past, his feet crunching on some of the steel chips that had missed the guard.

He stopped abruptly. 'Get your brush out, you lazy little bugger, this swarf ruins my shoes!'

'Okay! Okay!' replied Andy, then as the man walked away he muttered under his breath, 'and get stuffed George.'

'I'll brush up,' I volunteered. 'Where do you keep the brush?'

He indicated between the machines. 'Over there against the wall.'

Hurrying round I grabbed the brush and began sweeping vigorously, aware that eyes in the office might be watching. Something suddenly flicked the side of my neck and dropped inside my collar – and it was red hot! Dropping the brush I frantically tried to hook the thing out – and succeeded in pushing it further down! Even more frantically I bent double, almost doing a head stand in a desperate attempt to dislodge the burning tormentor but the thing easily evaded my wild wriggling and moved about at will to find a new patch of tender skin to lovingly sizzle against.

The sound of laughter rose above the hum of machinery.

'I liked your dance,' chortled Andy when, red faced, I eventually picked up the brush again.

'I don't know what happened,' I said. 'Something dropped inside my shirt and it was red hot.'

'A piece of swarf,' he informed me. 'It's dead hot when it comes off the machine, that's why it turns blue, you have to watch it. Got a piece in my ear once, it burned like bloody hell. I had to go to the surgery.'

I didn't like the sound of that and hurriedly finished brushing so I could get out of range of those vicious little red hot missiles.

Andy was taking the toolbit out to grind it when Chris stopped his machine and came over. 'It's ten past, we'd better get going.'

'Strewth!' said Andy. 'I forgot to tell him!'

Mystified, I stared at them. Chris explained. 'The newest apprentice has to get the foreman's tea from the canteen. It's been me – now it's you. Come on or we'll get caught in the rush!'

I followed him down to the toilets I'd passed on my way in, a dark, dismal place but at least it was clean.

Chris grinned as we washed our hands. 'I'm glad you've come, I was getting really pissed off collecting Sinbad's tea every day.'

'Is it a lousy job or something?' I asked.

He wiped his hands on a roller towel hanging on the wall. 'Oh it's not that bad but you have to keep your eye on the clock all the time so you don't get caught in the rush.'

I dried my hands, 'What's the rush?'

He laughed. 'You'll see 'cos we're late.'

We threaded our way through a flock of white-overalled ladies pushing trolleys, topped with shining tea–urns and turned, past the chicken run cloakrooms, and turned right into a roofless passageway. Along the right – hand side stood a long tank filled with bubbling, steaming liquid. A pungent smell drifted up.

'What's that?' I asked.

'Caustic,' said Chris. 'This is the back of the Plating Shop and don't put your hand in there or you'll have nothing left when you try and take it out.'

Then I saw the notice on the wall above: DANGER HOT CAUSTIC in large, red letters.

'What do they use that for?' I asked as we walked on.

'Cleaning metal. It's dead handy if you want something de-rusting, they'll always stick it in the tank for you, and up there,' he pointed to a line of windows above the tank, with an iron staircase fixed to the wall, 'is the Model Room.'

That sounded exciting. 'Is that where they make models?'

He laughed. 'Well what do you think they make in a model room? It's where they make all those big Meccano things you see in the shops. You want to go up there sometime, it's dead interesting, they assemble the Dublo engines up there as well. Up these stairs on the left.'

We climbed the short flight of wide steps and pushed through swing doors into the canteen.

I stopped short, astonished by the sheer size of the place. Rows of long, brown-topped tables and chairs seemed to stretch forever, and up in the spidery roof girders dozens of opportunist sparrows flew and perched and cheeped, filling the vast emptiness with their strident calling.

'Come on!' urged Chris, 'the hooter will be going any

minute and Sinbad will want to know why his bloody tea's late.'

We hurried across to a partitioned off area. 'The Staff canteen,' remarked my companion, 'for the bosses and office wallahs. They don't like eating with the common herd.'

This was my first experience of the inflexible 'them and us' attitude which prevailed throughout the Meccano factory – there would be more.

The Staff canteen was a total contrast to the rows of long, brown-topped rows outside. Small tables covered by pristine, white tablecloths with cups, saucers and plates were neatly laid out dotting the highly polished floor. On a long table by the door a tray with cups and saucers, a teapot, a jug of milk and a plate of toast was waiting.

'This is ours,' said Chris. 'Let's get going.'

And nervously aware of the tray's ultimate destination, I picked it up carefully and we set off across the canteen.

Disaster struck as we turned the corner by the caustic tank. A sudden, horrendously loud banshee wail erupted in the factory roof close by, making me jump so violently that the cups rattled and, before my horrified eyes, a piece of golden brown toast somersaulted gracefully to the floor! As 'up the road' in neon lights flashed across my mind, Chris picked it up, grinning at my ashen face.

'Don't worry,' he said, scraping the toast clean with his small, steel rule, 'they'll never notice. I dropped the lot once and had to go back for another load. Got a right bollocking off the canteen boss when I carted the tray of pieces in and another one from Sinbad for being late.'

'But ... but,' I stammered, still shocked by the enormity of my crime.

'Come on!' he urged. 'We're in the middle of the rush now

so you'd better watch it.'

Feeling slightly sick I carried my precious burden past the cloakrooms towards the main corridor. The noise of machinery had ceased and a different sound began to fill the air – a chattering, clattering rumble that swelled in volume as we reached and turned the corner – and I nearly had a nervous breakdown!

The corridor, so empty a few minutes earlier, was filled to bursting point with a hurrying bustling, cup waving, overalled and head-scarfed female tidal wave that bore down on us like an army on the rampage. There seemed to be hundreds, thousands, millions of them all intent on smashing my tray and its precious cargo to smithereens.

I was back round the corner in a flash – so was Chris – and we huddled against the wall as the juggernaut thundered past for its tea-break.

'Is that the rush?' I asked in quavering tones.

'That's it,' grinned my fellow refugee. 'They're only allowed to smoke in the passage so they all belt out here for their tea-break.'

The torrent slowed to a trickle. Chris poked his head round the corner. 'Come on, we're okay now.'

Cautiously I followed him, gripping the tray tightly. The entire passage was filled with girls standing chattering, smoking, eating, with cups balanced precariously on the window ledges. We threaded our way through the packed mass and reached the safety of the Toolroom with my tray intact. Just inside the door a trolley, topped by a tea urn, was parked with a white-coated lady dispensing tea and toast and sausage rolls to a queue of toolmakers.

'Okay,' said Chris, 'I'm getting a sausage roll, do you want anything?'

'No thanks,' I replied. 'But what do I do with the tray?'

He waved a hand. 'Just take it to the office they'll open the door for you.'

He went to join the queue and I went for my first meeting with Sinbad.

The Crown Jewels were never carried as carefully as I walked to the office. The door on the right hand side opened as I reached it to climb the two steps to the inner sanctum. Two men in pristine white coats were sitting by a long desk, while a pleasant faced man in a suit stood holding the door open. One of the white coats, who sported black, slicked-down hair and wore glasses, indicated the top of a filing cabinet. 'Just put it down there.'

I placed the tray with a feeling of profound relief and turned to go.

'So you're the new apprentice?' enquired black hair.

I almost shot to attention. 'Yes sir!'

He appraised me for a few moments then said, 'This is one of the best toolrooms in the country. A time-served Meccano toolmaker is respected anywhere in engineering, so while you're here work hard, learn, keep your nose clean and you'll be alright. Understand?'

'Yes sir.' I answered rigidly.

A slight smile twitched the stern mouth. 'On your way then.'

'Yes sir.' And thankfully I beat a hasty retreat to the safety of the shapers.

Two more apprentices were sitting on stools between the machines. Andy pointed to the swarf box in front of our shaper. 'I couldn't find another stool, you'll have to sit on the box.'

'Oh it's alright.' I said and perched myself precariously on the edge of the box.

He bit the end off the sausage roll and pointed with the remainder to the newcomers.

'This is Freddie. He likes playing with it, and if he's not playing with it he's thinking where he'd like to put it ... '

Freddie leered. 'That's what makes the world go round.'

'... and this is Stan, known as Stan to his friends.' The sausage roll pivoted in my direction. 'This is Roy.'

'How did it go with the tray?' asked Chris.

'Alright.' I said. 'They didn't say anything about me being late, but one of them, a guy with glasses on, gave me a bit of a lecture and told me to keep my nose clean – whatever that means.'

A chuckle rippled through the company and Stan said, 'What it means old son is that you toe the Meccano line, do as you're told and don't cause any trouble – or else.'

'Oh,' I said. 'Which one was Sinbad?'

'He was,' said Andy, 'the one with the glasses. The other white coat is Bill Jackson the foreman of the Tool Repair next door.' He pointed to the wall behind the shapers which had large, arched apertures along its length. Through these openings more machines and benches could be seen.

'Someone told me,' confided Freddie, 'that years ago, when old Frank Hornby first opened the factory, the Tool Repair was a stables.'

'Sounds like a load of horse shit to me,' cried Chris – and they all guffawed loudly.

'There was a bloke in suit,' I said. 'He opened the door for me.'

'Percy Hewitt, the Toolroom Superintendent,' volunteered Stan. 'Everyone likes him. He's always coming round asking how things are going, he likes everyone to be happy at their work.'

Andy finished his sausage roll and gave a grimace of distaste. 'Yuk! I don't know why I buy these things – they're bloody awful! I hope they leave some tea so I can get rid of the taste.'

Chris laughed. 'Well if they leave some toast don't eat it, our mate here dropped a piece on the floor.'

'They'll never notice the difference,' sniggered Freddie. 'It'll probably taste better with a bit of dirt on it.'

I breathed a silent prayer that he was right.

They began to talk amongst themselves, leaving me to look round at the vast array of machines now silent and motionless. Next to Chris's shaper was a tall machine, like a shaper turned on its end so the ram went up and down. Sitting by it, on a stool, a middle-aged man with sparse hair was reading a Daily Herald and chewing vigorously. The hooter suddenly wailed, not so close this time but still startling to my unaccustomed ears. Then the quiet of the tea-break began to recede as stools were dragged across the tiles and machines whined into life.

Feeling a bit like a spare part, I stood waiting for someone to tell me what I should do, but none of my companions seemed in a hurry to start work again. Freddie yawned loudly, stretching his arms above his stocky frame. He seemed to wear a permanent grin beneath his shock of spiky, black hair, in marked contrast to Stan who was tall with wavy, brown hair and deep set eyes which gave him a rather serious, unsmiling look.

'Bugger off Freddie,' said Chris, 'you'll be getting us told off.'

Grinning, Freddie gave a V sign and went off down the passage.

'Go and get the tray Roy,' instructed Andy.

Obediently I hurried to the office. The foreman was on his

own looking at a complicated drawing.

'I've come for the tray.' I announced nervously,

Without turning his head he waved a hand. 'And tell them not to be all day.'

With a gabbled, 'Yes sir!' I seized the tray and hurried down the steps.

'In here!' hissed Andy as I reached the shapers.

I skidded to a stop. 'What?'

'Bring the tray in here … Now put it down on the stool.'

Chris took the lid off the teapot. 'Good-oh. It's half full.' He poured tea into three mugs set out on top of his locker.

With relief I noted that all the toast had gone and taking a deep breath relayed the foreman's message. 'Sinbad said you're not to be all day.'

'That's bloody Freddie's fault!' said Andy savagely. 'I knew he'd get us a bollocking, hanging round like that.' He looked at me. 'Sorry Roy, you haven't got a mug have you?'

I shook my head. 'No.'

'Bring one in for tomorrow, 'cos Stan's had it now you've come.'

Stan shrugged and gulped his tea down. 'I'm off anyway. If Sinbad's in that sort of mood I'd rather be in next door out of the way.'

I watched him go, wondering about this rather strange ritual of the foreman's tea.

Andy took a last, hurried swig from his mug and tipped the tea-leaves into the swarf box. 'You'd better get that tray back to the canteen smartish in case Sinbad's on the warpath.'

'Are you coming?' I asked Chris as I picked up the tray.

He grinned and pressed the shaper's start button. 'Not on your life. I've finished with that caper – you're the foreman's tea lad now. Just leave it on the table you got it from.'

The long main corridor was almost deserted as I emerged from the Toolroom, the only sign of life being an elderly man in a bib and brace overall lethargically sweeping away the litter of fag ends, cigarette packets and bits of paper left by the rush. He winked as I passed. 'Tea up our kid.'

'Oh yes,' I rejoined with a quick smile and hurried on my way. As I came down the canteen steps the passage was suddenly illuminated by a baleful, flickering light. It came from an open doorway on my right. Curious, I peeped in. A helmeted figure, bent over a bench was doing something to a metal box on the bench and the intense light fizzed and crackled, sending grotesque shadows dancing madly across the workshop like tormented souls from some demon nightmare. The light ceased and the man straightened, pushing the helmet up. Then he saw me standing in the doorway. 'Don't look at the arc you young idiot!' He snapped. 'You'll get a flash across your eyes!'

'Sorry!' I blurted out, and fled back to the Toolroom.

Worried about a 'flash' I told the story to Andy. 'Bloody hell!' he exploded. 'Don't you know better than to look at a welding arc – it can take the skin off your eyes! You could end up in hospital!'

I felt sick. 'I didn't know,' I said shakily. 'Do you think I'll be alright?'

'Yeh, you'll be okay,' he said reassuringly. 'It was Chris's fault, he should have gone with you, the idle bugger.'

The terror of the 'flash' was soon banished by a growing fascination for the shaper. The effortless way the powerful machine sliced through steel was a joy to watch and the delight in working with metal, born on that first morning, has never left me. So I watched with envious eye as Andy so easily adjusted the stroke or changed the speed and once again set the machine in motion to transform a rough, misshapen lump of steel into a square, shining masterpiece. Would I ever be able to do as well I wondered as the hooter wailed and the machines droned gently down to their lunchtime silence. And in the sudden stillness voices called, chairs were scraped across the metal tiles and a growing murmur drifted in from the passage outside as the lunchtime rush thronged its way to the canteen.

'Coming to the bog to wash your hands?' asked Andy, and before I had time to answer he called Chris, who was fiddling with something on his machine. 'Come on bollocks! We're not on overtime you know.'

Chris came over, wiping his hands on a cloth. 'That bloody traverse keeps sticking, I'll have to ask Sinbad to get the Maintenance to have a look at it.'

Andy pulled a face. 'Rather you than me. He'll probably say it's your fault and he'd probably be right.'

Grinning, Chris flicked the cloth at him. 'Come on then, let's out amongst the crumpet and see if we can rub up against something soft that will make us nice and hard.'

'You wouldn't know what to do with it,' jeered his friend as they strolled towards the door.

I followed them out and was swept down the corridor by a slowly moving river of females who jostled against me on every side. I strove to keep my friends in sight and it was with some relief that I finally pushed my way into the noisy, crowded toilets.

Andy and Chris disappeared into the press of bodies as I pushed and squeezed my way over to the long unrinal trough – but it was a wasted effort. Every time I managed to start the system off somebody would bump against me and everything would abruptly stop again. After a few minutes of this start

– stop situation I gave up, hurriedly buttoned my flies and fought my way to the wash basins. Things were never like this at school!

Freddie and Andy were sitting between the shapers when I got back to the Toolroom. Andy indicated a vacant stool. 'Take a pew.'

'Thanks,' I said. 'I'll just get my sandwiches. Where's Chris?'

He waved a half eaten sandwich. 'He's got a can of soup on the furnace in the Hardener's and I'll bet he's lost his can opener – he always does.'

Through one of the high, arched openings in the wall I could see Chris walking back through the Tool Repair carefully carrying a can wrapped in a cloth. Freddie chuckled and quickly screwing his sandwich paper into a ball stood up and hurled it through the opening. His aim was straight and true.

'Oi!' cried Chris as the missile ricocheted of the side of his head.

With a satisfied smirk Freddie sat down and dusted off his hands. 'Bull's eye!'

Andy wagged a finger at him. 'One of these days,' he said, 'you'll clout the wrong person and get your face bashed in!'

The smirk widened. 'Not a chance – I'm too good a shot. I can knock a fly's balls off at fifty yards.'

Chris hurried up and set his can down on the locker. 'Ouch! That can's hot. I left it on too long and the bloody thing boiled. Good job I remembered to punch a couple of holes in the top.' He looked round accusingly. 'Who threw that ball of paper – it nearly knocked my bloody head off!'

'Roy did,' lied Freddie without batting an eyelid.

'Oh no he didn't!' exclaimed Chris as I began to protest

my innocence. 'If it's anything to do with balls it's always you, Freddie.'

Freddie sniggered. 'That's because I've got the biggest ones in Meccano.'

'And if you're not careful,' rejoined the victim sardonically, 'someone's going to get them in a vice.'

Freddie grinned and gave a deliberate V sign.

I chewed a sardine sandwich made for me by a worried mother who was firmly convinced that her beloved offspring couldn't last a day in a factory unless he was chock full of all the minerals contained in those tiny, oily fish.

Chris rummaged in his locker, fumbled in his pockets and looked perplexed. 'Anyone got a tin opener? I can't seem to find mine.'

There was a loud hoot of laughter as Andy smirked and held his arms out in triumph. 'Was I right, or was I right!'

Chris looked at the grinning faces. 'What's all this about?'

'I was saying before,' answered Andy, in a know-all voice, 'that you can never find a can opener to open your can – can you?'

'Oh. Ha. Ha,' came the sarcastic response. 'Well you're dead wrong this time 'cos I was just letting you make a prick of yourself, I had an opener all the time.' And from his trouser pocket he produced a battered Scout knife, complete with built in can opener.

We were fed and watered. Chris leaned over and dropped his can in the swarf box.

'You'll get a bollocking off Albert for that,' commented Andy.

Chris looked down his nose and puffed his chest out importantly. 'He wouldn't dare,' he said loftily. 'He's only the brusher-up and we're highly skilled apprentice toolmakers.'

Freddie sniggered, stretched his arms above his head and yawned loudly. 'Anyone coming for a walk to the shops?'

The others got up, pushing their stools against the locker.

'You wanna come, Roy?' asked Andy.

'No thanks,' I replied, 'if you don't mind, I'd like to have a bit of a look around.'

He laughed. 'You'll get plenty of that. Sinbad will have you running messages all over the bloody factory. See you later, and don't forget to clock on.'

'I won't,' I promised.

They strolled out. I sat for a few minutes gazing at the silent machines, feeling a rising sense of excitement. I was now part of Meccano, the most famous toymaker in the world. It seemed almost unbelievable that I was actually working in the very place where my own battered, but still cherished, Dinky Toys and Meccano sets were made so long ago. And as I sat alone on that small stool, fresh memories of desks and lessons, the rowdy playground and the ever-present shadow of the cane were suddenly swept away into the past by the gleaming, steel companions of my future.

I walked along the metal tiles to the end of the passage and looked across the room. It seemed that nearly everyone went out at lunchtime. Apart from a few isolated figures sitting by the benches reading newspapers, or quietly dozing, the Toolroom was empty. Eager now to delve deeper into the mysteries of my new trade, I wandered slowly along, stopping now and then to gaze at engineering drawings which, to my untrained eyes, looked so complex that it seemed miraculous how anyone could ever understand them. Lying on top of one drawing, which almost covered one bench, lay the long, unpainted casting of a steam engine.

Shining grey, with every detail standing out, it looked

more a work of art than a toy. Fascinated, I peered closely at the intricate moulding. Perfect, even to the rows of tiny rivets studding along the boiler, it was a masterpiece.

'Good isn't it?' said a voice.

Startled, I looked up. Nearby, a man, sitting on a chair, hands behind his head and feet up on the bench, was watching me. He had slicked back, brown hair, a small moustache and a friendly grin.

'Oh yes!' I said enthusiastically. 'It's fantastic!'

He gestured with a hand. 'Pick it up, Joe won't mind.'

Reverently I picked up the casting. It was surprisingly light, the bare, unpainted surface smooth as silk. I turned it over, wondering how ever anyone had ever gained the skill to make the tool that could produced this wonderful thing.

'Just started here?' asked the man.

'Yes.' I said, carefully placing the casting down. 'It's my first day.'

'You're lucky,' he observed. 'I know lads who'd give their eye-teeth to get a Meccano apprenticeship. How did you get in? Does your dad work here?'

'No.' I said, 'he's a mechanic at Bear Brand in Woolton. They make nylon stockings, but he served his time as a toolmaker.'

He chuckled. 'Works at Bear Brand does he, I'd better keep well in with you then, your dad might be able to get me some cheap nylons for the wife. She spends a fortune on the bloody things and they only last five minutes.'

Eager to please I said, 'Shall I ask him for you?'

He shrugged and got up. 'If you like. Well I'm going for a stroll before that hooter starts wailing.' Hands in pockets he sauntered off.

I wandered on, looking at the strange and unfamiliar

tools lying on the benches, the blocks of steel, shaped and drilled and polished. Unpainted Dinky Toy castings with pieces cut out for some unknown tool making purpose. On top of one of the many-drawered, wooden tool cabinets that stood at the back of each work-place, a Dublo passenger coach rested on a short piece of curved rail. I pushed it backwards and forwards with my finger, feeling how smoothly it moved along the rails. People were drifting back when a high pitched howl shattered the stillness. My God! The hooter, and I hadn't clocked on! Down the Toolroom I raced, skidding round the corners on the metal tiles and out into the corridor. Groups of girls walking slowly along hurriedly moved out of the way as I tore past them. A plaintive, 'Where's the bloody fire ejit!' followed faintly as I skittered round the cloakroom corner and up the final straight to that all important spindly-legged box. Skidding to a halt behind two men in boiler suits I seethed with impatience as they leisurely clocked their numbers. They moved away, I grabbed the pointer and swung it round to my number – 692. But wait a minute, this was the wrong place – I distinctly remembered Andy pointing to my number up on the left. It must be 629. Hurriedly I swung the pointer and poised, dithering over the hole. Was it 629? Supposing Andy had made a mistake and I committed the unforgivable sin of clocking someone else's number – I'd be up Binns Road before I'd hardly come down it!

A bevy of girls giggled up. 'Come on 'ansome,' sniggered one, cocking her curler-bedecked head. 'Lerra little gerl 'ave a go.'

'Sorry.' I mumbled, reluctantly stepping aside.

Bang! Bang! Bang! The three of them clocked on and giggled away up the passage.

I seized the arm again but it was no good, indecision had me in its grip. Oh where was that piece of paper with my number written down for all to see? I knew where it was alright – a thousand miles away in that locker by the shaper and by the time I got it I'd be late – and on my first day. The thought was so appalling that a suspicion of tears began to prick the back of my eyes.

'Ello, 'Ello, 'Ello' said a familiar voice behind me. 'Look whose fiddling with the clock then.'

I looked round into the grinning faces of Andy, Chris and Freddie. There was no time for excuses. 'I've forgotten my clock number!'

Reaching over Andy pressed the pointer into 629, then swung the arm and clocked his own number. 'Okay?'

I managed a grin. 'Okay, and thanks.'

He winked. 'All part of the service.'

As we walked back to the Toolroom the hooter suddenly erupted again. Starteled, I asked, 'What was that for?'

'The hooter?' said Chris. 'That's the end of the lunch hour.'

Puzzeled I said, 'But it went earlier.'

'Yeah,' he said. 'That's the warning – it goes five minutes before.'

Five minutes early! The words slowly sank in. I'd been tearing around like madman, thinking I was only seconds away from disaster and all the time I was five minutes early! So now I knew, but there was still a lot to learn.

Time meant nothing to me on that first afternoon as I watched and listened to my apprentice tutor. If it hadn't been for Chris, Sinbad would never have got his afternoon tea.

'Better wash your hands Roy,' came his voice above the noise. 'You've only got ten minutes before tea-break.'

Startled, I looked at the large clock above the passage

windows. 'Thank Chris,' I called gratefully. 'I'd forgotten all about it.'

He grinned over his shoulder. 'Don't worry, you'll soon get used to it.'

'Is it the same as this morning?' I asked Andy.

'Yeah, only it's biscuits instead of toast. You'd better get a move on.'

The sparrows were in great form as I hurried across the canteen, chirruping and whistling as they flew amongst the roof girders. Three trays rested on the table, all furnished with cups and saucers, a teapot and plates piled with biscuits. Which was Sinbad's? I looked through the open door into the staff section. A white, overalled lady was setting crockery out on tables at the far side of the room.

'Excuse me,' I called. 'Could you tell me which tray is for the Toolroom?'

'They're all the same,' she shouted.

'Thanks.' I called back, and mindful of the mornings near disaster, I picked the tray up with extra care.

A squadron of aerobatic sparrows escorted me back across the canteen, showing off wildly to their solitary spectator. I had almost reached the doors when something flashed across my field of vision and Sinbad's tea-break biscuits suddenly sported a coating of greenish, grey icing! For a horrified moment I was rooted to the spot, then I belted a crockery rattling path back to that life-saving lady in the white overall. The room was empty.

'Hello?' I called. No answer. I called louder. 'Hello!' Still no response and the precious seconds ticked away. Female voices sounded outside. I peeped round the corner. Two girls in green overalls were walking across the canteen towards me. They must be coming for the other trays – the ones with unpolluted biscuits. Slamming my conscience down I quickly exchanged plates and hurried through the door. The girls barely glanced at my guilty, red face as they chattered past and I was halfway down the steps when a plaintive wail rose up behind me.

'Oh Mary, them bleedin' sparras 'ave shit all over the biscuit!'

Like a thief in the night I crept away.

Most of the ill-gotten biscuits were still there when I collected the tray.

'Bloody hell! Look at this!' crowed Andy, as I appeared between the shapers. 'They've hardly touched the biscuits – and chocolate too.'

'Yum, yum,' said Chris, grabbing a couple. 'Tuck in Roy you're at your granny's.'

I looked at the small, brown squares and had a sudden, mental picture of the devastating result of the sparrow's messy dive - bombing. 'No thanks,' I said. 'I'm not hungry.'

Almost before the last echoes of the hooter's mournful wail had died away, the Toolroom was half empty. It was the end of the day for all my work mates, but for me, the new apprentice, it was the end of my beginning and I was in no hurry to leave.

'Coming to wash your hands?' asked Andy.

'Okay,' I said, and we strolled out to join the bustling throng surging down the main passage.

Scraps of conversation came to my ears ' ... see you later then Vera, and don't forget' '... I can't, I'm washin' me 'air' '... I'd 'ave soon told 'im if 'e'd said that to me!'

We crowded into the bog and pushed and shoved our way to the wash basins. More scraps of conversation. '... so I asked him who the hell he thought he was talkin' too' '... she does a turn that one.' '… Glad it's knockin' off time, I'm knackered!'

The passage was almost deserted as we walked to the cloak-room. 'Well, what do you think of Meccano?' asked Andy.

'It's good,' I said. 'No it isn't – it's great! I really enjoyed today, well most of it anyway. It wasn't much fun when that swarf dropped down my neck.'

He laughed. 'Yeah, that was a great dance you did, but you have to be careful when that stuff's flying about, it's bloody dangerous.'

'Where do you live?' I asked.

'Huyton. Not far from Chris. And you?'

'Woolton.'

He raised his eyebrows. 'The posh end eh?'

I flushed. 'No it isn't, it's the same as anywhere else I don't know why people think it's all posh and … '

Laughing, he punched me lightly on the shoulder. 'Don't get huffy, I'm just having you on. How did you get here?'

'On the bus.'

'Chris and I come on our bikes, he'll be waiting in the bike shed I suppose. We're usually halfway home by now but I didn't rush tonight 'cos it's your first day.'

'Thanks,' I said, feeling relieved that I had at least one friend to shepherd me through the first bewildering days in this vast, sprawling factory.

'What's your number?' asked my friend as we reached the clock.

'Six two nine.' I replied promptly. All through the after-noon I'd been repeating that number under my breath, I wouldn't forget again.

I lay in bed re-living my first day as a Meccano apprentice, the longest and most eventful day I could remember in all my fifteen years. The factory would be dark now, the raucous hooter silent, the dive bombing sparrows fast asleep. My mum and dad had listened with great interest – my older brother with less interest – as I recounted the day's happenings. Well, most of them anyway, the great, un-chivalrous biscuit robbery I kept to myself. And, as I hovered on the brink of sleep, the happy thought came that not only had I realised a childhood dream to work one day at Meccano, I was being paid for the privilege as well. It was a good feeling.

Finding My Feet

From far away a voice was intoning: 'Come on. You'd better get up, it's gone six o'clock.'

Drowsily I pulled the eiderdown over my head to shut out the sound. Whoever that voice was calling for at this unearthly hour it certainly wasn't me. I didn't have to get up until eight o'clock at the earliest. I drifted back to sleep, only to be rudely jolted into consciousness by someone persistently shaking my shoulder and my dad's voice saying: 'You'll be late if you don't get up. It's a long way to Meccano.'

In an instant I was wide awake. I wasn't going to school, that was gone for ever – and good riddance. I was a working man now. An apprentice toolmaker earning money, and this was the start of my second day.

A wash, a hurried bowl of Kellogs, a quick kiss for mum, grab my sandwich parcel and I was walking up the long hill to the bus stop with my dad: two engineers on their way to work.

'Goodbye dad,' and the warm, convivial, atmosphere of smoke and newspapers on the top deck of a number 81 bus. I had no newspaper or anyone to talk to, so I rubbed a small, clear patch on the misty window and watched the unfamiliar scene rolling past as the bus swayed rhythmically on its way.

'Next stop the Rocket.' The conductor's strident voice jolted me out of a doze and sent me hurriedly clattering down the stairs to the platform.

'Steady on!' snapped the conductor holding a uniformed arm out as a sudden lurch precipitated me down the last few stairs. 'Don't be so eager, our kid. We're not there yet.'

I grinned sheepishly at the blank, morning faces of the other passengers crowding on to the platform and wondered if they were also on their way to Meccano.

The next bus, going up Edge Lane Drive, was crowded and noisy with standing room only and I spent the short journey to Rathbone Road squeezed uncomfortably between a knobbly, khaki army bag and a large boiler-suited man smelling strongly of stale oil.

It was a good job I was getting off at Rathbone Road because most of the other passengers were, and I surged out of the bus between the army bag and the boiler suit with my feet hardly touching the ground.

The pavement was thronged with people, all hurrying in the same direction and the air was alive with the clatter of feet and the hubbub of conversation. The road was thronged too. Buses and cars, vans and motorbikes – side-car'd and solo, and push bikes streamed past in a noisy, endless procession. The world was on its way to work and so was I.

The Newsagent's shop, near the corner, was doing a roaring trade with a constant queue both in and out battling good-naturedly, or otherwise, for the right to use the narrow, congested doorway, and as I turned the corner into Binns Road the throng became a torrent – a tidal wave of bobbing heads that poured down that long, straight hill and in through the open factory gates. How different was this busy, vibrant scene to yesterday–a lifetime away now– when I'd walked so nervously alone down this same dark road to begin my long apprenticeship.

Dodging the traffic I crossed the road to the Meccano side. A cry of 'Hiya Roy!' rose above the tumult as Andy and Chris swept past on their bikes. I waved back, it was a good feeling being noticed by my new friends, and then I was swept in through the doors and down to a forest of waving hands in front of the clock. Muttering six-two-nine I pushed and shoved, cursing my lack of inches, until I managed to grab that elusive pointer and bang it decisively into my number. Mary's, Edna's and Teresa's seemed to be everywhere as I jostled my way into the cloakroom, and even there I had to push and wriggle through bodies to find my overall.

I finally reached the peace and quiet of the Toolroom at ten to eight to discover the shapers still deserted with no sign of Chris or Andy. They must have been talking somewhere. On their bikes they'd have arrived at the factory before me. I ran my hand along the cold, smooth, surface of the ram. Soon I'd be working the shaper on my own. Andy would be with Stan in the Tool Repair learning all about grinding. I'd have to learn quickly, it wouldn't do to have to ask Chris to help me all the time once Andy had gone. My hand touched the starter control box. Just one prod of a finger on that green button would instantly bring this silent machine into humming life. I pressed the button gently a few times, just to get the feel of things but somehow I overdid it and the motor suddenly began to howl, sounding incredibly loud in the quiet room.

'Switch that bloody thing off!' shouted a voice. 'It's not eight o'clock yet!'

Face aflame I hit the stop button and the motor droned into silence. A few minutes later my friends arrived. The hooter sounded and the Toolroom began its day.

About nine o'clock Andy said, 'Go and ask Sinbad for a requisition for a hand wiper. I'll take you down to get it and we'll see Cherrystone about your tallies.'

'Who's Cherrystone? And what are tallies?'

He laughed. 'Billy Cherry, he's the boss of the Toolstores. Everyone calls him Cherrystone, but not to his face – he'd go barmy if he heard you.' He fumbled in his overall pocket and produced a small, brass disc which he handed to me. A number was stamped in the centre and MECCANO LTD embossed around the edge.

'That's a tally. You get ten with your clock number stamped on them. Whenever you borrow a tool from the Toolstores you have to leave a tally; they put that in place of the tool so they know who's got what.'

'Oh I see,' I said. 'What did you say I should ask Mister Simpson for?' Somehow it didn't seem right to call the Foreman 'Sinbad' when I was only on my second day.

Andy appeared not to notice and said, 'Ask for a requisition for a hand wiper, he'll know what you mean.'

Dutifully I trotted past the whirring machines and knocked timidly on the office door.

'Come in.'

The Foreman was in a good mood, the enquiring face looked almost jovial as I stepped into the office. 'Andy sent me for a requisition for a hand wiper.' I recited.

Without speaking he reached for a small pad at the back of the desk, scribbled for a few seconds then leaned expansively back in his chair and, with an expansive gesture, presented me with the requisition. It was all rather unnerving, especially the way his glasses flashed in the overhead fluorescent light so you couldn't see his eyes.

Stammering a quick 'thank you' I bolted out of the office.

'Okay?' asked Andy.

'Yes,' I replied. 'He gave me the requisition alright but he never said a word and was sort of half smiling all the time – it was dead odd.'

He sniggered. 'He probably had a bit last night and was still thinking about it.'

'A bit? A bit of what?'

An incredulous stare greeted the question. 'A bit of the other of course. You don't know much do you?'

And he was right – I didn't.

We stopped at the Toolstores and, leaning through hatch, Andy rapped sharply on the battered steel covered counter with the edge of his steel rule. 'Shop!'

The room was huge and filled with long, high racks. Facing us, on the other side of a passage was a large desk stacked with boxes. A round, red face wearing glasses appeared above the boxes and said severely, 'Stop that knocking. We're not deaf you know!'

'Sorry Bill,' apologised. Andy. 'I thought you were all in the back. We need some tallies for our friend here. His name's Roy and he started yesterday.'

Bill Cherry came out from behind his desk and walked over to the counter, and as he approached it came to me that never before had I seen someone so aptly named. Small and round with a florid countenance he looked for all the world like a ripe red cherry. He came up to the counter, scrutinising me with bright eyes. 'So your name's Roy?'

'Yes ... er ... Bill.'

His face creased in a smile. 'Well I hope you're happy here and don't start giving a load of cheek like some people I could mention.'

'Aw Billy,' protested Andy, in a hurt voice. 'How can you say that about a nice lad like me? I've never given cheek to anyone in my life.'

'Humph!' snorted the store man. 'Some of us know different, and don't call me Billy. Now these tallies young Roy.

What's your clock number?'

'Six two nine ... er ... Bill.'

He wrote the number on a slip of paper. 'Right. If we haven't got them I'll get Mike to stamp some blanks up. Call back a bit later.'

'We're just going down to the other stores for a wiper,' said Andy, 'should we call on the way back?'

Bill scratched his head thoughtfully. 'Alright, I'll get Mike to do them now.'

As we passed the second hatch a loud shout of Mike! came echoing through the opening.

'Bill seems a nice bloke,' I commented.

'Yeah he is,' agreed Andy. 'Dead honest too – but he goes berserk if you start taking the piss out of him and he won't serve you – so watch it.'

The General Stores were further down the main corridor, past the turn off for the cloackroom – unknown territory for me. I handed in my requisition through the hatch to a girl in a green overall, who promptly gave me a small piece of edged, grey material, a bit like a dish cloth.

'When that gets dirty,' said Andy, 'bring it back here and they'll exchange it for a clean one. And make sure you don't leave it lying around – it'll be pinched for sure – and then you'll have to pinch someone else's, or get another requisition off Sinbad and a dead cert bollocking to go with it.'

I thrust the wiper firmly into my pocket.

My friend looked up the deserted corridor. 'Come on, I'll show you around a bit, but keep an eye out for Sinbad.'

Next to the stores was the Plating Shop. I looked in through the doorway. The whole place was wet with liquid overflowing from some of the long tanks and streaming away under wooden, slatted duck boards. A wispy vapour rose from other tanks as wellington'd men, protected by long, red shiny gloves and aprons, lifted baskets of brass, Meccano wheels from one tank to another. A pungent smell drifted through the doorway. I wrinkled my nose. 'Yuk! I wouldn't like to work in there.'

'Me neither,' agreed Andy 'and I'll bet their feet stink wearing wellies all day. Come on we'll have a gander at the Machine Shop.'

We crossed the corridor. My companion slid a door open, releasing a sustained, metallic drone. The noise came from lines of small machines busily working away, each tended by an overalled girl. Near the windows overlooking the corridor, men were operating long lathes that had round bars of brass protruding from the end. Metal boxes full of small components were dotted across the floor.

We stood just inside the doorway. I raised my voice above the din. 'What are they making?'

Andy shrugged. 'Bits for Meccano sets and trains, gear wheels and things like that.'

A white coated figure appeared from between the machines some distance away, walking purposefully towards us. 'Aye, aye!' exclaimed Andy. 'Time to get lost before we're asked what we're doing here.'

Nipping smartly back through the door, we beat a hasty retreat to the Toolstores.

My tallies were ready – bright brass with 629 stamped across the centre, and I watched with gloating eyes as they tinkled into my outstretched hand. 'Thanks Bill. They look like pieces of gold.'

'And that's a good way to think of them,' he said gravely, 'because they're a bit like that. With one of these you can borrow tools worth hundreds of bounds, so make sure you don't lose any. If someone gets one of your tallies and uses it to pinch something - you!' he pointed a stern finger, 'will be responsible for whatever's missing, and you may even have to pay for it!'

I clutched my metal discs tightly, imagining the sudden horror of finding one missing.

Andy reassured me as we got back to the shaper. 'Don't look so worried. Billy always gives a lecture like that, but as far as I know he's never asked anyone to pay for missing tools.' He started the machine. 'Come to that I've never heard of any tools going missing.'

But I was not so easily reassured and as the toolbit began its journey across the block of steel, I was once again furtively counting my tallies deep inside my overall pocket.

A week later I was working the shaper on my own and my tutor pronounced himself satisfied with my progress. I knew how to fill in my time sheet each day; how to use, well almost, a micrometer to measure critical sizes, I'd learnt about the buff coloured job cards and of the different types of metal, from lowly mild steel to high carbon HRS and the incredibly tough, toolbit smashing BKM, used in the manufacture of die casting tools. I'd met more of the other apprentices, (there were fourteen of us in all), been introduced to Lou Birch, who operated the big planer behind me that machined blocks which were too big for the shaper, and Fred Dodd, the slotter operator.

Fred was in his fifties, of medium height, thin and with his sparse hair carefully combed across the top of his head. He had a nose like a large, ripe strawberry, fleshy ears and the shiniest, black boots I'd ever seen in my life – and he was the young apprentice's friend. Eccentric in his ways, he would frequently be seen performing little dances round his machine or banging one shiny boot up and down loudly on the metal tiles in time to the slotter's oscillating movements. He was affectionately known as 'Doddy' and, despite his little oddities, he was a first class craftsman. The slotter was mainly used for cutting the shaped apertures in a press tools die, mainly the ones for Dinky Toy bases, as Andy confided.

Fred was able to machine a piece of metal so accurately that he could split a line three thousands of an inch wide. But machining was not Fred's only claim to fame – he was also the master of 'The Flourish.' This was a movement which began with the fingers and thumb of one hand held straight and together. The fingers were placed on a projecting part of the machine – a handle perhaps – then flicked with lightning speed to a series of other, different projections one after another.

The fingertips had to touch each target as they began, straight and together, but during the movement to each place fingers and thumb would flutter rapidly like a bird's wings in flight. The more targets and the quicker each target was touched, the better the flourish. During my time on the shapers I witnessed many attempts, including my own, to claim Fred's crown as King of the Flourish, but none of our efforts ever managed to surpass his speed and dexterity and he remained the undisputed champion.

Andy had little to do now I was operating the shaper, on Monday he would move next door to the Tool Repair to learn cutter and surface grinding with Stan, but he still kept a close watch on me from his relaxed position, leaning against the locker, where he was out of sight of the office.

'Tell you what,' he said, as I hammered the vice open to remove the piece of steel I'd just finished.

I looked up. 'What?'

He picked his teeth thoughtfully with his small, steel rule. 'You're going to need a long stand for that big block you're putting in next.'

This was news. He'd never mentioned a long stand before. 'What does it do?' I asked.

He picked a bit more. 'Oh it helps to support a big job like this – makes it easier to machine.' He raised his voice. 'Hey! Chris! Don't you think Roy needs a long stand for this big block?'

Chris looked over, grinning. 'Yeah! Definitely!'

'Okay,' I said. 'Where do I get one from?'

He pocketed his rule. 'The Toolstores. Just tell Bill you want a long stand, he'll know what you mean. And while you're away I'll start setting the job up for you.'

'Thanks', I said. 'Will I need a tally?'

He looked thoughtful. 'No, they don't bother for long stands.'

Two toolmakers were waiting at the hatch, talking. I craned my head round the corner. Bill was getting up from his desk. 'Who's next?'

'We're being done Bill,' said one of the men. 'You can fix this young lad up.' He moved over so I could reach the counter.

Bill's eyebrows raised enquiringly.

'Could I have a long stand please? For the shaper.' I asked.

Faint sniggeres came from my companions.

The storeman's face twitched. 'I'll see if we've got one,' he said, and disappeared between the racks.

'Just started here?' asked one of my companions.

'Yes. Last Monday.'

'Like it?'

'It's great. Really interesting,' I enthused.

A store lad came up and put a large drill on the counter.

'There you go Sammy.'

The man picked up the drill. 'Thanks Mike.'

Another lad appeared with a long wooden box which he handed to the other toolmaker. 'One height gauge.'

With a brief, 'Thanks Sid,' and a smiling, 'Hope you get your long stand okay,' to me, they departed.

Bill came back, his face twitching. 'I can't find it,' he said gruffly. 'I'll get Mike to have another look – Mike!'

A tall fair-haired lad came round the corner. 'Yes Bill?'

'This lad's come for a long stand for the shaper, see if you can fix him up will you?'

Mike grinned – everyone seemed to be grinning today. 'Okay Bill, I'll see to it.' He strolled off down the passage as Bill disappeared behind his boxes.

So I waited ... and waited ... and waited. Nobody came. Had they forgotten all about me? Finally I called timidly, 'Bill.'

No answer.

I tried again, knocking gently on the counter. 'Hello?'

No response. Then Mike came round the corner, grinning from ear to ear. 'Well you've been here for ten minutes, have you enjoyed your long stand?'

And it finally dawned on me, as I felt the colour rising in my cheeks, that I'd been set up, the victim of an obviously well known joke. I grinned back sheepishly at the store lad. 'It was a joke?'

He nodded. 'That's it. They all fall for that one.'

'Very good,' I said. 'I'd better get back now – after my long stand.'

'Tara,' said Mike.

The Golden Eagle Lays My Egg

A nother week had sped by. I was settling happily into working life and as the days passed feeling less and less of a newcomer and more one of the lads – and today had the added excitement of my first pay-day.

Last Friday I'd watched enviously as my friends returned from the long queue, gleefully opening their wage packets and even more gleefully counting out the contents. I'd been left out then but, now I'd worked my week in hand, one of today's small, brown envelopes would have my name on it. I'd already decided not to open the precious packet in the Toolroom, but to carry it home in triumph so my family could share in the excitement of the grand opening.

It was heady stuff this pay-day business. A different atmosphere was abroad in the factory, an air of expectancy as the day wore on and reached a climax when the long queues signified that, in factory language – 'The Golden Eagle was about to shit!'

And I was already feeling that air of expectancy when I went to collect Sinbad's morning tea tray.

'Ah Byrne,' he said as I picked up the tray. 'When you come back I want you to deliver this jig to the foreman of the Train Room.'

I almost dropped the tray! I knew all about the Train Room even though I had only been working at Meccano for a short time. It was the place at the top of the factory where train carriages rails and Dinky Toys were assembled. Hundreds of girls worked there, sitting by long conveyer belts, and from my gleeful workmates, I'd heard every gruesome detail of the fate awaiting a young virgin apprentice if he ventured into that lair of female sex maniacs.

'Tie you up they do,' gloated Freddie. 'Then they pull your trousers down and stick you on a conveyer so they can all laugh at your plonker waving in the air as you go past.'

'And remember that lad from the Maintenance,' Chris had chirped. 'They took his trousers off and wouldn't give them back and he had to hide behind a load of boxes for hours!'

I'd rocked with laughter at these stories of some unfortunate lad's humiliation. Now it was my turn! I didn't drink my share of the tea and I didn't tell the others of my impending doom – they'd only have laughed and dredged yet another gory tale of some poor lad's downfall, and before very long they'd have the story of my humiliation to add to their list.

The only thought I could console myself with as I trudged back from the canteen was that at least I was wearing clean underpants. My mother was always very particular about this: 'In case you have an accident.' Well, so far I hadn't been involved in any accident but my spotless, white underpants could soon be on their way to something infinitely worse!

Sinbad gave me a small, metal plate with a number of steel pegs projecting from it and clamp at one end.

'Give it to Mister White, he knows what it's for. Do you know where the Train Room is?'

I knew all right, and was it my imagination or was he smiling to himself.

'Yes sir, I know where it is.'

'On your way then.'

Feeling sick with apprehension, I walked slowly down the long mile of metal tiles and turned right through the door. Girls seemed to be coming and going to the toilets at the end of the Press Shop, most with their hair in curlers and wearing head scarves. They looked a cold-blooded gang. 'Just the type to drag a young lad's trousers off and tie him on a conveyer belt,' I thought bitterly.

Like a condemned man I dragged myself past a big pile of boxes on the right and suddenly I was on the edge of a vast, open space. Practically as far I could see were lines of conveyer belts moving slowly along, dotted with bits of Dinky Toys, railway carriages, rails and other parts. And hundreds – no, it must be thousands – of girls, were sitting, busily working, on either side of the conveyers laughing and calling to each other.

My stomach sank to my boots as I searched desperately for a white coated – figure. They wouldn't dare touch me if I could make it to the foreman. 'Where are you mister white in white?' but there was no humour in the thought. Music suddenly blared out from loudspeakers in the roof; that would drown my cries for help – if I managed to make any. Then I saw him, miles away at the other end of the room and, taking a deep breath, I plunged recklessly into battle and ran the gauntlet of the conveyer belt snipers!

'Oo! Isn't 'e luvely Mary, I'd like to take 'im home for the night!'

'He's from the Toolroom – I wonder warris tool's like!'

'Cum over 'ere Sampson an' lerrus feel yer muscles!'

Crimson faced, I charged on through a barrage of double meanings, giggling cat-calls, and downright dirty remarks until, breathless and mortified, I reached the white-coated oasis. But even there I wasn't safe. Those Train Room girls didn't give a fig for authority.

'Bring 'im over here Ronnie,' carolled a sharp faced girl in a red turban, 'and we'll give 'im some lesson in riveting things together!'

Mister White raised a pair of harassed eyes to heaven as shrieks of laughter rose above the music. 'You wouldn't like to swap jobs would you?'

'Er no,' I said lamely, holding out the jig. 'Mister Simpson sent this. He said you would know what it's for.'

He took the jig. 'Thanks, and will you tell him we're having trouble with the Dublo rail clenching tool again and could he send someone to have a look at it.'

'I will,' I promised, thankful from the bottom of my heart that I was too inexperienced to be sent on that errand back into this den of terrifying females.

Curbing an urge to ask the foreman to escort me safely to the end of the room, I once again plunged recklessly into the fray. The Dinky Toy gunners had reloaded.

'Here 'e comes again! Get your knickers off quick Doris!'

'Isn' 'e cute – I'll bet he's still a virgin!'

On I went, trying to appear not bothered, but when I heard a strident: 'Let's gerrim on the conveyer and see warr'es made of!' My nerve snapped and I was almost running when I finally left the hoots of laughter behind me.

Subsequent visits to the Train Room followed much the same pattern, but none of those sharp tongued girls ever attempted to lay so much as a finger on me, and as I grew older and more adept at flinging my own witty remarks in retaliation, the terror of the Train Room dwindled and eventually died away altogether.

I was quite cock-a-hoop when I went with our group up to the shops on Rathbone Road at lunchtime. 'I had to go up to the Train Room this morning,' I announced casually.

'Did they rip your trousers off?' asked Freddie excitedly.

Boasting: 'Nah, they never bothered me. I had to take a jig to the foreman, from Sinbad, so I just strolled up there, gave him the jig and strolled back again – the girls never bothered me.'

Andy looked at me cynically as we turned into the Newsagents. 'Just strolled back eh? Not bothered at all? You were strolling so fast, with your panicky red face, that you didn't even see me on my way to the top bog.'

Chastened, I let the subject drop.

With every click of the shaper's traverse my pay packet came nearer, and I was in a state of high excitement as we settled ourselves for the afternoon break. Freddie was toying with a small, flared tube of black plastic, turning it over and over in his fingers as we talked. Curiosity finally got the better of me, I asked, 'What's that Freddie?'

He looked down at the tube. 'Oh this? It's a watchmaker's eyeglass. I got it a couple of weeks ago – it magnifies things. All the toolmakers have them to see marking out lines better.'

I was intrigued. 'Can I have a look?'

'Sure.' He held it out 'What you do is sort of screw it into your eye tightly so no light gets in. When you get really good you can keep it in your eye without holding it.'

Intent on showing how good I was I screwed the flared end firmly into my eye-socket but it promptly fell out on to the floor.

Chris picked up. 'You'd be no good as a watchmaker – have another go.'

I did, with the same result, so I just held it and examined my fingers through the powerful lens. 'Wow have I ever got dirty nails, I can see all the little lines on my fingers. This is a terrific little thing I must get one of these.'

'Yeah,' said Andy. 'Now you're getting paid you can join the Tool Club.'

I gave the glass back to Freddie. 'What's the Tool Club?'

They all had huge grins, and Freddie was positively smirking. Was there something funny about the Tool Club?

'You pay so much a week,' grinned Andy, 'a bob or two each week and when your turn comes round you go to the shop and get some tools. You pay for forty weeks so if you put in a bob in you get two quids worth of tools, two bob a week and you get four quids worth, and so on.'

'I'd like to join that,' I said, 'but there's nothing funny about it, so what are you all grinning about?'

Chris laughed. 'It's just that you looked so funny trying to screw that eye-glass into your eye. I almost expected the thing to come out of the back of your head with an eyeball inside.'

To show I could take a joke I laughed myself. 'I suppose it must have looked funny at that.'

'It did!' they roared.

The hooter went, bringing my pay-packet ever closer. As I collected Sinbad's tray I noticed a smear of vivid blue on my finger. Odd, I wondered where it came from? When I got back to my still grinning friends, I cleaned the mark away with my wiper and promptly forgot about it in the excitement of the count-down to the pay- queue.

Then, at last, the clerk carrying the precious box came through the small door in the corner of the Toolroom. The machines droned to a stop and I took my place in the lengthening queue. As we shuffled forward, I listened to what the other men said; it wouldn't do to make a mistake when I announced my claim to that precious packet. Clock number, followed by name was the correct procedure, so I practised under my breath as the line moved forward. Then, suddenly it was my turn. 'Six two nine, J.R. Byrne.' I said confidentially to the young clerk, who promptly started sniggering down his nose. He was still sniggering when he handed me the packet.

Bloody nerve! What was he giggling at? He wasn't much older than me anyway. I'd always thought there was something a bit odd about people who worked in offices and never got their hands dirty and this sniggering little twerp dishing out our wages had proved the point. But the clerk's peculiarities couldn't dampen the thrill of finally getting my pay-packet and I walked proudly past the queue – the sniggering, smirking queue – back to my machine. I tucked the envelope carefully in my locker, wondering at all this mirth that seemed to be about on pay-day. There was no doubt about it – getting money certainly did funny things to people.

The last part of the day seemed interminable, but eventually the hooter announced that we could all go home for the weekend. There was no waiting for my friends tonight. I didn't even bother to wash my hands in the hurry to get home and show my trophy to my family. Grabbing my coat I fought a vigorous battle through the crowd to the clock and legged it up the road to the bus stop. And the pay-day syndrome even seemed to have affected Liverpool Corporation bus crews, for as the conductor took my fare he grinned broadly and asked: An' how was werk today blue eyes?'

'Alright,' I answered, wondering what he was on about.

Down the long hill I hurried, quietly let myself in, hung my coat up and, with my pay-packed held out proudly in front of me, made a dramatic entrance into the living room. 'Evening all – I got paid today.'

Whatever response I expected it was definitely not the one I received as all heads turned in my direction.

My brother burst out laughing. My mum shrieked, 'My God! What's wrong with his eye!' My dad smiled knowingly and picked up his cup of tea.

'My eye?' I exclaimed, startled. 'What's the matter with it?'

'Look in the mirror you nitwit,' cackled my unfeeling brother.

I went over to the mirror above the fireplace and it was my turn for a shock. Completely encircling my right eye was a broad, vivid blue ring. I rubbed vigorously and it smudged all down my cheek. I stared uncomprehendingly into the mirror, where on earth had all this stuff come from and what was it?

My dad had served his time as a toolmaker and he enlightened me. 'Engineer's Blue on an eyeglass at a guess.'

And it all became clear. Freddie fiddling with the eyeglass, tempting me; my grinning friends; the wages clerk; the pay queue; the bus conductor and God knows who else. I flushed hotly as the pictures raced through my mind. I'd be a laughing stock on Monday. How was I ever going to face them all again?

My dad must have read my thoughts. 'Don't worry,' he chuckled, 'they'll have forgotten all about it by Monday.'

I fervently hoped he was right.

And it was dreadful stuff to wash off, that Engineer's Blue. Like some hideous, contagious disease it contaminated everything it came in contact with and by the time I'd finished in the bathroom the soap, the towel and even the wash basin had all aquired a faint, but very definite tinge of blue!

'What is Engineer's Blue?' I asked my dad when I eventually came down stairs.

He got up. 'Come on, there's a tin in my old toolbox in the shed, I've had it for years.'

After a bit of rummaging in the box the small, round blue tin was located and when he levered the lid off the paste inside glistened dark and evil in the torch light as he explained its use. 'The stuff it's made of is very fine. You smear it on bearings or a piece of metal which has to be perfectly flat and slide it over a special, flat surface plate, any high spots remove the blue so then you can remove them.'

'I see,' I said. 'I wonder if my eye has any high spots?'

He chuckled. 'You were lucky. One place I worked at they used to initiate new apprentices by pulling their trousers down and sloshing Engineer's Blue all over their privates. The poor lads would end up in a hell of a mess I can tell you.'

A shiver ran down my back. This was the second time today that forcible trouser removal had come within my working orbit. It seemed that, as far as the factory world was concerned, an apprentice's private parts were communal property. I hoped my mum continued to keep my underpants in pristine condition – the watchmaker's eyeglass might only be the beginning!

But through the haze of Engineer's Blue, and the lurking threat of losing my trousers, shone the bright light of my weekly pay packet and the new-found affluence it would bring. My mum had other ideas.

'Ten bob!' I protested stridently. 'That's nearly half my wages!'

'I think that's very fair,' she said mildly. Other lads have to give more than that - a lot more. You're working now and it's only right that you should pay a share of the bills. Try living on your own and see how far you get on ten shillings, it would hardly pay for your food, never mind the rent and the gas and the electric ... '

'All right,' I said, reluctantly handing over a ten shilling note. 'Here you are.' And in my heart I knew that, compared with some of the stories I'd heard, I was getting off lightly. Some unfortunates were ordered to hand over their pay-packets intact, relying on their mothers' generosity to see them through the week. At least I was being allowed to manage my own financial affairs, but visions of a new, light-weight sports bike were rapidly fading.

*

The weeks rolled by, putting healing distance between me and that pay-day Friday of humiliation, and my dad had been right, it was forgotten about by Monday. My trousers stayed up but the Engineers Blue returned for a lurid encore. This time it was all over the handles of my machine and I was covered in the stuff before I realised where it was coming from. After that it became second nature to carefully wipe all the handles when I returned to my shaper.

I joined the Tool Club, (at the low rate of a shilling a week), and another sixpence a week made me a member of the Social Club. With these commitments, plus my mother's share, I couldn't afford the luxury of travelling by bus every day, (I was no longer given the fare from the family coffers), so my old bike was hauled out of the shed, oiled and tinkered with and pressed into daily service.

It weighed a ton did that old Raleigh, and no matter which direction I was travelling in, the wind was always against me. When it rained, and I had to wear my huge, sail-like cape, I'd totter into the factory after a six mile ride that, seemed more like sixty, soaked with sweat and completely exhausted.

Most lunch times, when the weather was fine, I'd go for a stroll with my friends, usually up to the shops on Rathbone Road, although we rarely bought anything – we were invariably broke. When rain prevented this constitutional, we would drift up to the main entrance by the clock where we'd stand, courageous in our in our numbers, wolf whistling and making loud, facetious remarks as the girls streamed in.

Mostly we were ignored but occasionally a comment would goad the victim into retaliation and a furious, 'Why don't you bugger off and play wit the traffic!' would be hurled back at us, instantly invoking a chorus of jeers and cat-calls from our tightly packed ranks.

But working in Meccano was still an exciting novelty for me and occasionally I'd stay behind in the almost deserted Toolroom to wander along the benches, looking at the mysterious, intricate tools, the parts of trains and Dinky Toys and pieces of Meccano that lay about on the work places. One of factory's products most widely seen in the Toolroom was the large, can-like base for the signal for the 'O' gauge clockwork railway sets. By every toolbox at least one of these round containers could be seen, up-ended and filled with screws, bits of metal and all manner of odds and ends.

Pay days came and went and suddenly there was talk of Christmas. We were to have two days off, Christmas Day and Boxing Day, but weeks before the actual event the festive spirit began to permeate through the factory. Toolmakers with a leaning towards the stage could be could be seen reading scripts instead of newspapers as they prepared for their roles in Meccano's Annual Pantomime and the normally tranquil atmosphere of the tea-breaks was periodically shattered by enthusiastic voices raised in bawdy Pantomime songs. The captive audience responded to this desecration of their tea-break with a vigorous barrage of loud jeers and insults, which grew in volume until the budding opera stars gave up the unequal contest and went back to quietly learning their lines.

Members of the 'Boozers Club', run by Sam Brown, the cylindrical grinder operator in the Tool Repair, could be heard gloating about the prospect of becoming 'pissed as a newt' when they finally received their long awaited liquid assets, which they'd been paying for all year at so much per week, on Christmas Eve.

The factory began to take on a seasonal look as the girls fixed bits of tinsel and small Christmas decorations to their machines and work places. Christmas was coming and the toymakers were welcoming it in with open arms.

But it was when the tickets for the Meccano Christmas Dance went on sale that the festive season really got under way. Held at the huge Grafton Rooms in West Derby Road, the Christmas Dance was the factory's social event of the year. Interest in the opposite sex, always prevalent in the Toolroom, suddenly rocketed to new heights as the more attractive girls were marked down for personal attention at the Dance. Discreet enquiries were initiated to discover the intended victim's boy-friend, or marital status so that precious time and, more importantly, precious money, would not be wasted in the prolonged wooing of the unavailable.

And it wasn't only the male population who were making plans. As the date of the Dance approached, curlers and head-scarves were abandoned wholesale in favour of elaborate hair styles, lipstick and mascara. The traffic past the Toolroom windows increased steadily as the girls abandoned the top toilet for a trip down the corridor which took them past as many males as possible, and it was almost impossible to venture out into that passage without bumping into a bevy of eyelash fluttering Christmas Dance hopefuls. Even the normally aloof office girls were not immune to the Dance fever, sallying forth from time to time to stiletto - heel their way through the parade of lesser mortals with self conscious superiority.

My friends were in a state of high excitement after hearing, from the older apprentices, the ease of making conquests at the Dance. The lurid details of what could be in store when the strains of the Last Waltz died away had them almost turning somersaults with lustful anticipation.

But the wave of Christmas Dance hysteria flowed over me with scarcely a ripple because I wasn't going.

'You're not going!' exclaimed Chris incredulously. 'All that talent just begging for it – and you're not going! You must have lost your bloody marbles!'

Sheepishly I hammered the vice handle tight and trotted out my excuses. 'Well I'd hardly know anyone, I'm too young to drink, I can't afford it, and I can't dance – so what's the point?'

For a few seconds he digested this statement, then said gently, like a teacher addressing a particularly thick pupil, 'The point is, old son, that there'll be about two thousand drooling bits of crumpet just waiting to get their knickers off. Kenny was telling me the other day – you just can't go wrong.'

'I could,' I said banging the block of steel down in the vice. 'It's not my scene Dave. I've never had ... ' I stopped short as someone in a white coat came out of the office. 'Look out! Here's Sinbad!'

He scuttled back to his machine as the foreman advanced towards us – and stopped at the shaper.

Head down, but surreptitiously watching the two figures from beneath lowered eyelids, I busily wound the traverse handle to take the job under the toolbit. I couldn't hear what was being said but from Chris's attitude and his pale face, it was a safe bet that he was being given 'a right bollocking'. I wound the handle furiously, hoping I wasn't next on Sinbad's list. I was lucky, escaping with a curt – 'Less talking!' fired at my lowered head as the foreman continued on his way.

Although the excuses I'd given to Chris were all true, the main reason which I kept to myself, was that in the company of girls I was painfully shy. It was one thing to call smart remarks from the middle of an apprentice gang, but the mere thought of being shut up in a dance hall surrounded by hordes of man–hungry females had me quaking at the knees.

Besides myself it was also Chris and Andy's first Meccano Christmas, and although Freddie and Stan had been working at the factory, they'd missed the previous Dance. They weren't going to miss this one and, if my friends had anything to do with it, neither was I. 'You should go,' they argued, because even though I was the youngest and newest apprentice I was included as one of the lads, therefore it was my duty to join all the other members of the fraternity in having a whale of time as the whole crowd of us lustfully sampled all the delights on offer at the Dance. They were wasting their time; my fear easily eclipsed any sense of loyalty and I clung tenaciously to my decision even when persuasion was eventually abandoned in favour of ridicule and derisive remarks.

But as the big night drew nearer, enthusiasm began to wane. The Dance ceased to be the sole topic of conversation and if the subject was raised it would precipitate a crop of slightly worried expressions. I began to suspect that the much quoted 'the more the merrier' slogan was, in reality, a confidence boosting safety in numbers. Despite all the earlier bravado, it appeared that I was not the only one to be attacked by the jitters at the prospect of being closely confined with the cream the Meccano talent for hours on end.

I started to feel a certain smugness when the worried expressions deepened as the lads tried to decide what to wear, what time and where to meet, and what was the best way to ask a girl to dance. None of these problems bothered me in the least – because I wasn't going.

On the Friday before the big event a deep air of melancholy hung over our afternoon tea break.

'All set for tomorrow night?' I asked, happily breaking the brooding silence.

The response was immediate and short. 'Drop dead!'

'You know,' said Andy, to nobody in particular, 'for two pins I wouldn't bother going to the bloody Dance. All the fuss and palaver. It'll probably end up being a bloody dead loss anyway.'

There was a gloomy murmur of agreement.

'I mean,' he continued, 'what chance do we have with the talent, when all the older fellas start flashing their money about? I'll only have a quid and that won't go very far on a bird who wants to drink rum and pep all night.'

More gloomy murmurs were lost in the wail of the hooter.

On Saturday night I went to the local cinema, known as the 'Bug House,' with some friends, to guffaw loudly at 'Abbott and Costello Meet the Invisible Man.' The evening was helped along by periodic, mental pictures of the lads, standing in a nervous, forlorn little group at the edge of the dance floor, watching the big spenders twirling past with the cream of the Meccano talent cradled in their arms. And serve them right! After all the snide comments I'd had to put up with, they deserved a miserable evening.

Well, I couldn't have been more wrong, because, far from having that miserable, wasted evening – they all had the time of their lives!

But I was unaware of this outcome as I waited on Monday morning to witness the miserable post – Dance faces, smugly listen to the grumbling of what a lousy affair it had been and a complete waste of time and money. Pleasant phrases flitted through my mind: snide, sarcastic, own-back jibes. 'What a shame you spent all that money and had a lousy time.' Or, smirking. 'Are you all going again next year?'

To my chagrin, the crop of jubilant, happy faces coming through the door on that frosty morning didn't look at all as if their owners had had a lousy time. Unable to contain my curiosity I asked, 'How did the Dance go?'

'Fantastic!' enthused Andy. 'Absolutely, bloody fantastic! You don't know what you missed – isn't that right Chris?'

Grinning from ear to ear Chris agreed. 'It sure is. I've never been to a do like it. You should have seen the crumpet there. We had a belting time and we all got fixed up, didn't we Andy?'

'We sure did,' smirked his fellow Dance-goer. 'How did you go on with that red-head with the big tits?'

'Great! Good job she lived near me, I didn't get home 'till half one. She works in the Model Room. I'm seeing her again on Saturday. Her name's Alison. How did you go on with that blonde?'

'Nearly two o'clock for me. She was like a bloody octopus. After I'd taken her home I had to walk back, it must have been about four miles. I was knackered when I got home.'

'Are you seeing her again?' asked Chris.

'No. she doesn't work here and I don't fancy a four mile walk when I've taken her home.'

Right up to the hooter they went on and on about dancing the Hokey Cokey, and bouncing up and down because the dance floor was sprung. And how people bought them drinks all night, and the place was awash with gorgeous girls in low-cut dresses, and how you kept getting flashes of thighs, suspenders and even knickers above the stocking tops when skirts flared out as the girls spun round on the dance floor.

It sounded out of this world, and while all this had been

going on I was watching a daft film in our local flea-pit. I'd missed the opportunity of my young life!

Andy clapped me expansively on the back. 'Next year, old son, we'll all be there – you included.'

I vowed I would, and I was, and I had a whale of a time – but that's another story altogether!

Christmas Comes But Once A Year

Christmas was finally here, or at least the morning of Christmas Eve, and although the factory was working it was a very half-hearted affair. The big rush was over, production targets met, and now we were in festive mood. All over the world the Dinky Toys, Meccano sets and Hornby Trains which had poured down the lines of conveyer belts, where hidden away. In countless wardrobes, cupboards, lofts and next door neighbour's houses the toys from Binns Road waited for Father Christmas and the breathless delight of Christmas Day. It was a good feeling to know that I'd helped a little in weaving this timeless magic.

And some of that magic had clung to me with the promise, from my parents, to help me out in my efforts to buy a new bike. As soon as the holiday was over I could go to Cundles, huge cycle shop in Liverpool and choose my own bike, (within a certain price limit!) I already knew what I really wanted as I'd seen my dream bike in the window of the store. A light-weight Claude Butler, bright maroon with drop handlebars and Deraillieur gears was just waiting for me to come and buy it. No more would I puff and pant, cursing under my breath as I laboriously pedalled an old ton weight along. On my new, lightweight racer the daily ride to work would be an exhilarating dream of power and speed, culminating in a triumphant sprint down the crowded hill of Binns Road. And at the weekends I'd be off, far from the smoky city, flashing along the quiet lanes of Wales, or spiralling gloriously down the long, winding hills of the Lancashire Dales. But that was in the future, today we were all off to the pub for a lunchtime Christmas celebration.

'Come on!' urged Andy, as I stuffed a sandwich into my mouth. 'You haven't got time for that, we can eat later. We've got to get to the pub early or we'll never get a seat.'

'I don't know about this,' I mumbled worriedly. 'Bloody hell, I'm only fifteen and I've never been to a pub in my life.. Supposing the law comes in and catches us – we'd be in dead trouble then.'

Chris grinned. 'You can hide behind me if you're that bothered. Now let's get going!'

Binns Road was crowded with pedestrians who all seemed to be going in different directions. A group of girls with tinsel in their hair were dancing along singing a discordant, and irreligious version of a well known Christmas carol.

'Oh come all ye faithful, we're all goin' to the p . u . u . u . b!'

Freddie rubbed his hands together gleefully. 'Look at all that crumpet. They look half pissed already, and they haven't got to the pub yet!'

The Railway was on the opposite side of the road, midway between Meccano and Crawfords and although we were early we didn't get a seat, in fact we were lucky to get in the place – it was practically bursting at the seams with laughing, overalled factory workers, pouring the Christmas spirit down their throats almost as fast as they could tip the glass. With me nervously bringing up the rear, we pushed and elbowed our way into a corner. I looked round. We were surrounded by giggling, cigarette puffing girls, but in between the packed bodies I caught glimpses of fawn, overall coats and faces I recognised from the Toolroom.

Chris smacked his hands together. 'Right! What are we having? Pints of bitter all round?'

Andy and Freddie nodded assent. I tried to recover from the shock. Pints of bitter? They must be mad! We were all under drinking age, and not just under – years under! If the police came in we'd all end up in jail; well they would, I wasn't risking it.

'I'll have a glass of lemonade.' I announced.

'You bloody well won't!' snorted Andy. 'We're celebrating Christmas and you can't do that on lemonade!'

'But we're under age,' I protested, 'and I'm even more under age than you lot. What happens if the law comes in? We'll be for it then, and—'

'Keep your voice down, you bloody moaner, or we'll be kicked out before we've touched a drop!' hissed Chris.

'Yes but ...' I began, then stopped under the intimidating glare of three accusing faces. The odds were definitely stacked against me, so I capitulated. 'Okay. I'll have a glass of whatever you're having.'

'That's more like it,' grinned Chris, emphasising the point with a friendly punch on my arm.

'Money out!' ordered Andy. 'A shilling each for us and sixpence for Roy.'

As we sorted our money out, a loud voice rose in song above the general hubbub. "Four and twenty virgins came down from Inverness, and when the ball was over there was four ... "

'CUT THAT OUT!' Roared an even louder voice from the direction of the bar.

Amidst hoots of raucous laughter the singing died away. We looked at each other across our outstretched, coin-bearing hands.

'Well?' queried Andy. 'Who's going to get the drinks in?'

'Freddie!' decided Chris, promptly. 'He's the oldest.'

'But I don't look it,' retorted Freddie, with a smirk.

'Yes you do!' interjected Andy. 'Especially with that scruffy overall. Come on Freddie, they won't serve any of us – that's for sure.'

A worried expression replaced the smirk. 'Supposing they ask how old I am?'

'Lie through your teeth, like you usually do, and tell them you're eighteen, said Chris, 'and if you don't get a move on the dinner hour'll be over.'

Freddie shuffled his feet uncertainly.

Chris pressed home the point. 'I don't know what you're worried about anyway, at the Dance you spent half the night standing at the bar swigging, you weren't worried about your age then.'

'That was different!' retorted Freddie, with spirit. 'I had my suit on then, it always makes me look older.'

Andy sighed wearily. 'Well if you won't go, what are we going to do? We can't just stand here without a drink, some smart arse is bound to notice and then we'll be for it.'

'We could have lemonade,' I ventured.

Incredulous eyes swivelled towards me.

'Drop dead!'

Chris's face suddenly lit up. 'Hang on! Give me the money quick! I can see Jimmy over there he'll get the drinks in for us.' He excused his way through our cordon of girls and disappeared in the crowd.

Five minutes later he was back with a beer-swimming tray. 'How's that for service?'

'Good lad,' crowed Andy, lifting his glass, and here's to Jimmy.' He took a long gulp and smacked his lips – 'Lovely!'

We took our glasses. Chris leaned the tray against the wall. 'We'll keep that for later.'

Freddie raised his drink. 'Happy Christmas.'

Our glasses were raised and clinked together. 'Happy Christmas,' we chorused.

I swallowed my first ever mouthful of beer. The slightly sour, malty taste wasn't what I'd expected, but the stuff was definitely drinkable.

In that warm, smoky, noisily friendly pub, we talked, cracked jokes and eyed the talent – and suddenly our glasses were empty.

'Money out lads,' said Andy, cheerfully. 'Time for another round.'

Freddie frowned. 'I'll just have a half this time, the bloody stuff seems to be bloating me up!'

'Me too,' agreed Chris. 'I'll just have a half as well.'

'Chickening out eh,' jeered Andy. 'Can't stand the pace? Well I suppose I might as well have the same. So it's four halves of bitter.'

For all his scornful words he looked quite relieved to be able to join the half pint brigade, and it occurred to me that perhaps the professed seasoned drinkers were not so seasoned after all.

More girls pushed near us and the smoky air became scented with heady perfume. Freddie sniffed appreciatively. 'Cor! Smell that. It's enough to get anyone feeling randy.'

Chris eyed him cynically. 'You're randy all the time, playing with yourself through your trouser pocket.'

Freddie leered, rattling his money about. 'Just checking my loose change, that's all.'

Chris snorted derisively. 'And if you believe that you'll believe anything ... look out, here comes Andy.'

We could see our tray-bearing friend threading his way carefully through the press of bodies. As he reached the ring of girls a blonde, standing nearby, called out, 'Hiya Andy!'

He looked startled. 'Oh hiya Mary,' adding superfluously. 'I'm just getting the drinks in.'

She laughed. 'In that case we'll have four rum and peps.'

Andy grinned back. 'And you could have 'em, only we're all just about skint.'

A mocking, drawn out *Aaaahh* came from the group, was followed by a typical Liverpulian offering from a pretty girl with dark hair. 'You're breakin' me heart. Hang on while I go an' rob the poor box in Saint Teresa's for ya.'

'We'd take it too!' retorted Andy.

She made a face. 'You're quick.'

'You've got to be working in Meccano!' came the prompt reply.

I couldn't help thinking what I'd have said in the same situation. On past performances – very little.

'Was that the Mary you took home from the Dance?' I asked, as Andy came up.

'Yeah. I took her to the pictures as well, but she didn't seem keen. She's eighteen and I think she's got a boyfriend.'

As we took our drinks Freddie asked casually. 'Did you get anywhere? She's got a lovely pair of tits.'

Andy took a sip of his drink and looked at the questioner disdainfully. 'Mind your own bloody business, you sex starved bugger!'

Freddie grinned lecherously.

And I realised that I too was grinning, and that a feeling of well-being was slowly permeating through my body. The world seemed a much rosier place now than it had half an hour ago when I'd trailed nervously down Binns Road. I took a long drink, gazing benevolently at my laughing friends over the top of my glass. What a grand bunch they were, these Meccano apprentices. So friendly and helpful, they'd welcomed me into their ranks without a moment's hesitation. Now I too was one of the lads, and it felt great.

A voice broke into my reverie, raised above the general din. 'Here you are then. As you're all so 'ard up we've bought you a Christmas present.'

Mary was holding out a tray, on which reposed four small glasses of dark liquid.

'Didn't I tell you they were lovely girls,' beamed Andy. 'Who says there's no Father Christmas.'

'Go on then,' laughed Mary. 'Take the bloody things. I can't stand 'ere all day.'

We took the glasses with loud thanks to our female benefactors.

'What is it?' I whispered in Chris's ear.

He sniffed the drink and grinned slyly. 'It's only blackcurrant.'

I grinned back – I couldn't stop grinning. 'Oh that's all right then, I like blackcurrant.' I held the glass towards Mary and her friends and called, 'Happy Christmas girls.'

They held their glasses up. 'Happy Christmas lads.'

Happy Christmas!' shouted my friends, waving their glasses in the air.

I took a festive swig of my Christmas present. The dark liquid slid down like sweet nectar – and seared my stomach like sulphuric acid! I gasped and coughed, trying to catch my breath, then, hurriedly gulped down the remainder of my beer in an attempt to put out the fire. I jogged Chris's arm urgently. 'You said it was blackcurrant,' I croaked.

'So I did,' he roared. 'I forgot to tell you it was probably mixed with a bloody great dollop of rum!' And he went off into peals of laughter.

I began to laugh. I couldn't stop laughing. In all my fifteen years I'd never realised that the world was such a funny place, and not only was it funny – it was rapidly becoming absolutely hilarious!

'What's the joke?' cried Andy. He too was grinning, and Freddie. The pair of them were beaming like a couple of over-alled Cheshire cats.

And it was catching, this beaming business, everyone was at it. Wherever I looked the faces were beaming happily or laughing uproariously and the noise was becoming almost deafening. I drained my glass. There was no sulphuric acid this time, so I had another go in case I'd missed a drop. And standing up was becoming a bit of an effort, so I leaned against the wall – somehow managing to bang my head in the process – and watched Andy, my bosom buddy, telling an hilarious joke to a laughing circle of lads and girls. The voice of the singer rose above the clamour: *'The vicar's daughter she was there she had us all in fits, jumping off the mantle-piece and landing on her ...'*

'CUT THAT OUT!' roared the loud voice. *'YOU'LL BE OUTSIDE NEXT TIME!'*

Then someone began singing Silent Night, and the whole place took up the carol. I weaved my way over to my friends and we stood, arms round each others shoulders, belting out the words. And when the final 'heavenly peace' died away we cheered ourselves hoarse.

Mary looked at her watch, 'We'd berrer get back, it's nearly clocking on time.'

'Bugger the clock!' I heard my voice say. 'Let's shtay here.'

'Oo. Listen to 'im,' giggled the dark haired girl. 'Swearin.'

She looked lovely so I put my arm round her and crooned, 'How about a Christmas kiss, gorgeous.' At least that's what

I thought I said but she didn't seem to understand, and responded with a startled, 'Yah wah?'

My bosom buddies understood because the roared, 'Give him a Christmas kiss Doreen!'

She turned her head. 'Gerroff!'

'Are go on,' I coaxed. 'Just one liddle kish.'

'Gerroff!'

'Mean!' cried the buddies in unison.

The victim's face flushed. 'Oh orite – but just one.'

She turned her face and I kissed her. Even through my alcoholic haze her lips were soft and moist. I could smell her perfume and feel the warm thrust of her breasts against me. It was a moment of Christmas magic I would never forget, but only a moment, she pushed me away in embarrassment. 'That's enough. Don't make a meal of it.'

'I wouldn't mind.' I said seriously, but she'd turned away.

I looked round. All my friends were at it too. Snogging away as if time – and the clock – didn't exist.

Then we were all dancing back up Binns Road, arm in arm and singing and floating back from somewhere in the crowd ahead came the faint, but audible words of a different song, 'The village magician he was there, his tricks were all a farce, he pulled his ... '

He was still at it.

The main corridor was loud with shrill voices, laughter and snatches of off tune Christmas carols as the tinsel, holly and mistletoe bedecked girls thronged back to work.

Outside the Toolroom three large balloons, suspended at head height, jigged up and down invitingly as the string was jerked from the other side of the Toolroom windows. Most of the throng wisely gave these inviting targets a wide berth but, for two young revellers, the temptation proved too great.

Giggling and calling to their friends, they dashed up and simultaneously prodded the balloons with their cigarettes – and, accompanied by shocked squeals, the laughing faces disappeared in a dense, white cloud. The balloons had been filled with French chalk powder.

We fell about with mirth as two blanched faces slowly emerged from the cloud. From their shoulders up every vestige of colour had vanished, even their hair was white! Without doubt the spectacular success of the trick must have exceeded the perpetrators wildest dreams.

Still giggling, although without much mirth, and to the accompaniment of shrieks of laughter from their workmates, the victims continued on their way, vainly trying to brush away their coating of clinging, white powder.

Laughing hysterically, we weaved our way through the door and flopped down on the stools between the shapers as the hooter added its strident voice to our laughter.

And for all the effect it had that afternoon, the hooter might as well have saved its metallic breath. Long after the final drones had died away most of the laughing, talking groups of toolmakers were still laughing and talking as if that imperious summons had never sounded. Quite clearly the Toolroom was not in the mood for work and the noticeably absence of shock waves radiating from the Press Shop, indicated that the rest of the factory was feeling much the same.

The lunchtime parties and the general holiday atmosphere were excuse enough for this abnormal behaviour but, as far as the members of the Toolroom were concerned, there was an additional reason for their happy, couldn't-care-less attitude. It lay in the innocent- looking mugs residing on benches, by toolboxes, on locker tops and perched precariously on parts of machines. No shining urn had filled these mugs this Christmas Eve, their precious contents had been gloatingly poured from bottles hidden away in drawers, lockers, under benches and other secret places. The Boozing Club had finally delivered the goods!

From early morning, through one of the openings into the Tool Repair, I'd seen Sam Brown visited by a constant procession of smiling toolmakers. A brief look at Sam's list, followed by a careful rummage through cardboard boxes under nearby benches, resulted in a paid out member joyfully departing with a suspicious-looking bulge under his overall. The Boozing Club members were happy at last – with the prospect of being happier still as the afternoon wore on.

But in the midst of all this merriment there was at least one individual who had no interest whatsoever in sampling the contents of those suspicious bulges smuggled into the Toolroom – I wasn't feeling very well at all.

Not long after we'd returned from the pub, I'd left my shaper looking as if it was working, (one of the few machines that was working), and retired out of Sinbad's view to eat the rest of my sandwiches. It was a big mistake! My stomach, already trying to cope with an unaccustomed diet of beer and rum and black current, decided that the addition of oily, sardine sandwiches was just not on and lost no time in passing on the message. The noisy, hilarious, singing and laughing world of the lunchtime booze-up had suddenly become the morning after, eighteen hours too early!

Chris galloped up, flushed and happy. 'Guess where I've been?'

Preoccupied with my churning innards, I hadn't noticed he'd been away. 'Where?' I asked disinterestedly.

'Up to the Train Room. They're playing music over the

Tannoy and the girls are dancing on the conveyers, pissed as newts.'

'I hope they fall off,' I said sourly.

He looked at me closely. 'Are you alright?'

I grimaced, 'I've got bad guts.'

'Mine are alright,' he said happily.

'Lucky you. I feel awful.'

He thought for a moment then said knowledgeably, 'It's snogging with strange birds in the pub - you've caught something.'

'Don't be daft,' I retorted, with more derision than I felt. 'You can't catch something that way ... can you?' wincing as another cramp gripped me.

He looked at me narrowly. 'You might have caught a dose.'

My heart skipped a beat. 'A dose? A dose of what?'

Hands spread in a gesture of the obvious, he enlightened me. 'The pox! The clap! You know.'

I did, but very little, and I wasn't letting him know how little. 'Balls! What a load of tripe! You can only catch the Pox if you have it off with a girl – and anyway you were snogging in the pub as well.'

'Not with Doreen I wasn't,' he smirked, 'and I feel alright. You were the only one who got in a clinch with her.'

And he was right! Now I was going hot and cold. My God! What had happened to me? I'd never touch alcohol as long as I lived – but how long would that be? I put up a brave front. 'That's a load of bollocks. Doreen's a nice girl. It was mixing rum and beer that did it. It's just bad guts, that's all.'

'So you hope.'

And he was right again, so I hoped – fervently!

Sinbad's appearance in the office doorway sent him scuttling back to his machine, leaving me with far more to worry about than simply having a cement mixer in my stomach. After our recent conversation I hoped the foreman was on his way to give my pitiless friend a right bollocking for talking – I was disappointed. Sinbad had caught the Christmas spirit and, smiling benignly, he strolled round the room, stopping now and then to chat to individuals who were smiling too, and far more benignly than he was.

As the mugs tipped more frequently so the level of noise increased with much laughter and calling to distant friends, but in the vicinity of the shapers, most of the racket was generated by our slotter operating neighbour Doddy, who kept practising wildly executed clog dances on the metal tiles with his heavily studded boots. This racket did my throbbing head no good at all and I wished I could ask him to pack it in. But I didn't dare, because as the youngest apprentice, I was at the very bottom of the Toolroom's pecking order and had no right to ever question the behaviour of a senior worker, even when he was acting like a complete lunatic.

I managed The foreman's afternoon tray without incident then joined my friends between the shapers.

'How are you feeling?' asked Chris, solicitously, grinning from ear to ear.

I ignored him. 'I'm going to have a sit down in the bog.' I said in response to Freddie and Andy's questioning looks. 'I'm not feeling too good.'

Loud laughter followed me through the door and I suspected that Chris was relating his version of the reason why I was under the weather. In the world of the male adolescent there was little sympathy for self inflicted wounds.

Jostling my way through the packed, noisy girls in the corridor, I reached the blessed peace of the empty toilets and went into the dark end cubical next to the wash basins. Closing the door I gratefully sat down, leaning my throbbing head against the cistern pipe. It wasn't the most comfortable of seats, the lid having long since disappeared, but at least I was away from the racket in the Toolroom.

I must have dozed off for a sudden noise intruded on my senses, causing me to look around, momentarily not realising where I was. I listened. Silence except for the sound of muted voices in the corridor. The noise must have been someone going out. I closed my eyes again, then heard a furtive scuffle and the sound of stifled laughter. Fully awake now I listened, suspiciously. Something was happening on the other side of that door and I had an uneasy feeling that it concerned me. Suddenly, with a great roar of water, the toilet flushed! In panic I leapt up to see a hand withdrawing from the swinging chain and three gleeful faces peering down at me over the top of the wall.

'Merry Christmas!' yelled the mirthful trio into my startled face.

There was indeed little sympathy for self inflicted wounds.

Maybe it was the sudden shock, or perhaps my bout of feeling rotten had run its course, but whatever the reason, as I came out to see the happy chain-pullers jumping down from the wash basins, I realised that my headache had gone and the maelstrom in my innards had quietened down to a gentle gurgle.

I was seized and spun round so the joyful jokers could see the result of their brilliant plan, the sight of my wet trousers reducing them to hysterical bundles draped over the wash basins. But I didn't care a jot! I was myself again and one of the lads and a wet backside was a small price to pay for that.

Boisterous with self importance we bragged and cat-called our way through the massed clamour of Christmas corridor girls to the noisy haven of the Toolroom.

With the foreman's tray I collected the news that the management had decided the workers could all go home an hour early and be paid. Glad tidings of great joy indeed, which I carried abroad to Meccano's tippling toolmakers like a Yuletide town crier, leaving in my wake a trail of accelerated, determined assaults on the last few drops of the Boozing Clubs festive spirit.

And in our joyful thousands we Meccano-ites thronged and jostled down the passages, along the corridors and past the redundant clocks until, wildly Happy Christmasing everyone in sight, we surged through the open gates to Binns Road and home.

*

Although only weeks had passed, the festive season already seemed a distant memory. Youth looks forward to the exciting future, relegating the past to the fireside of advancing years. But I retained one tangible link with that first Meccano Christmas, my sparkling Claude Butler bike. With the promise of increasing my share of the repayments, I had managed to persuade my family to bring the purchase date forward, and my excitement knew no bounds when I arrived at the shop to collect the precious bike That bike was all I'd dreamed of and each morning I'd speed down that long, crowded hill feeling like the winning rider in the Tour de France.

Life was good. The halcyon days rolled by and it seemed that nothing could mar my carefree world. Then I was told about the apprentice's initiation ceremony!

It was Friday afternoon and I'd been on a message for Sinbad to the Model Room. I always enjoyed going up there, it was quiet and bright from the light of the windows over-looking the canteen roof. Fixed to benches along the walls were small, interesting machines for magnetising the Dublo engine electric motors and checking the electric circuits. In the centre of the room, girls sat at large, flat tables fitted with Dublo rail lay-outs, checking the performance of the engines by pulling lines of trucks and carriages. I'd never had an electric train set, we couldn't afford it, and would watch in fascination as those splendid models of the Duchess of Athol, the Duchess of Montrose and the streamlined blue of Sir Nigel Gresley whizzed so realistically round the track. I longed to have a go but never had the nerve to ask.

At the far end of the room the elaborate models were constructed from Meccano sets for shop displays. Huge windmills, Blackpool Towers and Fairground roundabouts, ablaze with miniature lights, could often be seen resting on the work tables. The models I used to build at home never looked like these intricate, working Meccano masterpieces.

As I got back to my machine Andy came over to the open arch looking in to the Tool Repair. 'You've got to give me a hand emptying the wet grinder tank,' he called. 'Come on in.'

I waved acknowledgement. 'I'll be there in a minute. I'm just helping Albert with the swarf boxes.'

Albert was the Toolroom labourer and he was waiting impatiently for the contents of my swarf box to be emptied into the large box on his trolley. One at each end we lifted the heavy, wooden box, over-turned it on top of the box on his trolley and set it down on the floor again. Albert hooked his thumbs through the straps on his bib and brace overalls and cocked a jaundiced eye at the pile of swarf, orange peel, decaying apple cores, fag ends, bits of paper and half flattened soup tins.

'You can bloody well cut this out,' he grumbled. 'There's

a bin by the door for this stuff. I've got to pick all this out before I empty this lot into the scrap bin. You bloody apprentices just don't care.'

'It wasn't me Albert – honestly,' I protested. 'All the fellas just dump it in there when I'm not around,' which was not strictly true, but near enough.

He snorted in disbelief and pulled out a packet of Players. There was only one cigarette left and after extracting it, he casually dropped the empty packet into the pile of swarf, before pulling the trolley to Chris's machine, where the little drama was enacted all over again. As far as the contents of our swarf boxes were concerned Albert ruled – O.K!

The wet grinder was in the far right-hand corner of the Tool Repair, near the windows of the Hardening Shop. It was a big machine, about seven feet tall, with a long steel-encased table containing a large magnet to hold the work in position. The grinding wheel was like a giant, inverted cup. Water was pumped down the centre of this wheel for cooling and when the machine was in operation, with the table travelling backwards and forwards, clouds of spray swirled into the air and settle about the operator, dampening his overall. Dwarfing us small apprentices, it was an intimidating machine which none of us looked forward to operating.

Andy was round the far side, were the dartboard was fixed to the wall. The tank was about three feet square and the same in height, and he was baling the water out with a can and pouring it into one of a number of five gallon drums standing on a trolley.

He looked up irritably. 'About bloody time! I've nearly finished the job on my own.'

A slight exaggeration, as only one of the drums was half full.

'Sorry mate,' I apologised, 'I had to help Albert. He was moaning his head off about all the other stuff in the swarf boxes.'

He snorted, derisively. 'I'll bet he's been doing that for the last thirty years.'

Sniggering, I rolled my sleeves up and began baling with a spare can. The water was filthy with grinding dust – and it stank! I wrinkled my nose in disgust. 'Bloody hell it stinks. How often do we have to do this?'

'About every three months,' replied my fellow sufferer. 'I've only done it once before, and if you think this stinks, wait 'till we get to the sludge at the bottom - that's bloody vile!'

As the water level dropped we had to reach further into the tank, receiving the full benefit of the malodours, stagnant reek.

'God!' I exclaimed, after a particular good nose – full. 'I wouldn't like to fall in this lot. You'd stink for a week!'

My friend gave a gloomy look. 'You might have to. They grab you and dump you in here upside down for your initiation.'

Initiation! A word dreaded by apprentices the world over. A word which instantly conjured up nightmare visions of suddenly being grabbed by a jeering mob and publicly subjected to all manner of unspeakable indignities.

The can slipped from my grasp and fell to the floor with a clatter and a trickle of evil-smelling black mud. I picked it up and asked, 'Have you been ... ' I forced myself to say the dreaded word, '*initiated?*'

He turned his mouth down. 'Not yet. It usually happens when you move in here, or at dinner time when it's raining and they're looking for something to do – the bastards!'

I made a mental note to stay out of the Toolroom on rainy

lunch times. The initiators, whoever they where, weren't going to find me an easy victim.

'Still,' continued my friend, 'it could be worse I suppose. In some places they pull your kecks down and blue your balls.'

I shivered, remembering my dad's account of that particularly degrading treatment.

From then on, as we baled and scraped and slugged, my vivid imagination had a field day, and by the time the tank was finally emptied I'd been initiated in every in every way possible and a dozen more besides. In less than an hour I had degenerated from a whistling, happy-go-lucky apprentice into jittery, watchful nervous wreck!

We shovelled the more solid sludge into the bin then pulled the trolley, with its foul, sloshing cargo, down the main corridor and through a door between the men's and women's toilets, into another passage. Below a long row of small, grimy louvered windows of the female toilets, a tap was fixed to the wall above a large grid. Andy stopped the trolley.

'Here we are. We pour it all down here and help to fill the Mersey.'

And down it went, mud and all. As we tipped the drums, watching the dark, oily liquid swirl sullenly away through the iron grating, I felt a certain satisfaction; those initiation bastards weren't going to stick anyone's head in that lot!

As the drums were filling up with clean water I asked Andy where the passage went.

'It goes to the Boiler House,' he said. 'We'll go and have a look one day, it's dead interesting. There's a massive diesel generator that they put in during the war so the place could keep going when the electricity went off, at least that's what the boiler man told me. They start it up sometimes and it makes the floor vibrate like bloody hell. They didn't make toys then of course, it was stuff for bomb sights and things. Joe Swarbreck has a real smart casting hanging over his bench from a tool he made during the war.'

His words evoked vague memories of wailing air-raid sirens; and lying in the Anderson shelter, which my dad erected in the front room, as the throb of aircraft engines vibrated through the house. Of the far-off thudding of bombs in the city and anti-aircraft guns and the lights suddenly going out. And pressing my nose against the window of the corner shop in Woolton Village, that sold Reece's milk in square bottles, gazing with futile longing at the glorious display of Hornby Trains and Dinky Toys that were – as a notice said with cold finality – NOT FOR SALE.

A voice broke into my reverie. 'Give us a hand.'

I held them out. 'Which one?'

'Both of them you bloody idiot!'

We lifted the last, brimming drum onto the trolley, sloshing the water over the edge and down my trousers and into my shoes. My friend had fared much the same way with the previous drums.

At last the tank was full again. Andy performed the final act of pouring in a small can of hot water, mixed with soda crystals to prevent rusting, and we were finished. Wet and dirty I looked down at the slowly subsiding ripples and wondered whose head would be forcibly plunged into that placid surface. Whoever it was could comfort himself with one, small consolation, as he emerged coughing and spluttering from the depths – at least the water was clean!

The Great Laxative Job

As the days passed without a mob of wild-eyed, cackling initiators descending on me – or anyone else for that matter – I ceased to jump at every shadow and the spectre of the wet grinder tank began to recede. By Friday it had gone completely and I was whistling again. Sinbad and his cronies were in great spirits when I went to collect the morning tray, laughing uproariously at some private joke.

'We hope you lads enjoy your tea,' chuckled the foreman, as I picked up the tray.

'Oh ... er ... thank you,' I said, wondering what he was going on about.

I dumped the tray on the stool. Chris lifted the teapot lid and gave an exclamation of delight. 'Look at this! Almost a full pot! The buggers have hardly touched it!'

'Sinbad said they hoped we enjoyed the tea,' I said. 'I wonder why he said that?'

'It's obvious,' declared Andy. 'They've finally realised that we deserve it more than they do. Where's your mug?'

Brim full were our mugs er that teapot was empty, and Chris proposed a toast to our benefactors. Raising his mug he quoted facetiously: 'For what we are about to receive, we of the common herd do extend our humble thanks to the ruling class of Meccano's Toolroom.'

'Hear! Hear!' we jeered, and raising our mugs in mock salute, we took a large gulp.

Had we the least suspicion of what devious treachery really lay behind that enticingly full teapot, we wouldn't have touched the contents with a ten foot pole. But we had no reason for suspicion so, smugly congratulating ourselves, we drained our mugs to the last drop.

Sometime later, after I had returned the tray to the canteen, I began to feel uncomfortable, with much bubbling and churning in my nether regions. The feeling rapidly descended to an area which necessitated a hurried stop of my machine and an even more hurried gallop to the toilets.

With every muscle below the waist tightly clenched to avoid total catastrophe, I burst into the life-saving dimness – to be faced by rows of tightly closed doors. Frantically I hobbled along thumping on each door and pleading loudly: 'Hurry up fellas! This is an emergency!'

From behind those doors the unsympathetic responses were hurled back. 'Serves you right!' ... 'Piss off!' ... 'You want to lay off the booze then!'

As I waited in agony, with beads of sweat breaking out on my forehead, the outer door slammed open and an ashen faced Andy struggled in. Without preamble he stated his problem. 'I've got the shits!'

I nodded and muttered through clenched teeth, 'Me too!'

Moving his legs only from the knees down, my fellow sufferer did the round of door thumping. The responses were much the same as mine.

Afraid to talk in case the effort unleashed something totally beyond our control, we huddled against the wall, listening to the rustle of the newspapers being read behind the doors, and each in his own private world of cold sweats and rapidly tiring muscles.

Then, after an agonising eternity, the glorious sound of a toilet flushing. I didn't see who the life-saver was but I nearly knocked him flat in my haste to get into that blessed cubicle.

And as I sank gratefully down onto that still warm seat, I heard the outer door slam open again – I only needed one guess to know who that was. The door thumping and shouting began again but, as far as I was concerned it was wasted effort, necessity dictated that I tenant that cubicle for some time!

More flushing noises, followed by the sound of desperate scrambles, announced that my friends had at last achieved their bowel's desire, and in the ensuing minutes the term frequently used for the toilets as the Thunder Box was emphatically proved to be thoroughly justified. And in our explosive symphony we had an appreciative audience, whose loudly voiced comments could be heard during a lull in the proceedings. The one I shall always remember came from an obvious newcomer to our fan club, who guaranteed his place in history with a startled: 'Good God! What's going on here – the Meccano farting contest!'

Finally plucking up courage, I left my refuge and managed to reach the Toolroom door before having to beat a hasty retreat – wordlessly passing a white faced Andy on the way. At the next attempt I made it to my machine but couldn't stay long enough to switch it on. This time I passed Chris's ashen face.

And that was the pattern of the rest of the day for my friends and I, passing each other either on the way up or on the way down, like pale and restless ghosts. I managed to keep body and soul together long enough to do my bit with Sinbad's afternoon tray; my appearance causing much ribald amusement in the office – although no further comments were made concerning the morning tea.

Tired and worn out, we listlessly dragged our bikes from the racks, generally agreeing that the days nerve-racking events were entirely due to: 'Those bastards in the office lacing the tea with fucking laxative!'

That bike ride home was the longest and most uncomfortable I'd ever known, but I made it - just. Then, without touching my tea, I went wearily to bed for an early night.

We never quite decided on the reason for – as it came to be called – The Laxative Job.

Was it our foreman's way of putting a stop to the time-honoured tradition of the apprentice's tea? We never had the courage to risk drinking it again. Or was it simply that Sinbad and Co. sported a wicked sense of humour? At the distance of many decades I am inclined to think it was the latter. After all, even the bosses are entitled to have their little joke.

Albert rolled his trolley to a stop by my machine. 'Here's another little job to keep you busy,' he announced, taking out a packet of Players.

I looked down at the array of steel blocks. There was a lot there, so it must be a die-cast tool, and that meant most of those blocks would be incredibly tough, toolbit annihilating BKM.

I picked up the buff coloured job card and my heart sank. It was a die-cast tool for the new Centurion Tank, so I would spend half my time on the shaper and the other half on the grind stone repairing those wrecked toolbits.

'Bloody hell!' I said in disgust.

Albert blew a stream of smoke towards the roof. 'Heard about the new apprentice?' he asked airily.

I hadn't. Not a whisper. 'No! When's he starting?'

He smirked with satisfaction at being the first with the news. 'Monday morning.'

'We haven't heard a word,' I said. 'How did you find out?'

The smirk broadened with even more satisfaction and he tapped the side of his nose significantly. 'Aha! that's my secret.

There's not much goes on around here that I don't know about.'

A very true statement. At times it seemed positively uncanny the way our labourer knew about various goings-on long before the rest of us had heard so much as a peep. MI5 had certainly lost out when Albert came to work at Meccano.

We unloaded all the smaller blocks, the larger pieces for the main body of the tool, being too big for my machine, were passed on to Lou Birches planer.

I felt slightly depressed by Albert's news. It heralded a change and the end of the old order. Chris would go to the grinders in the Tool Repair; Andy would come back into the Toolroom to learn the small Dekel miller, the bandsaw and the bench lathe; Stan progressed to the large horizontal milling machine and Freddie to the large centre lathe. I stayed with my shaper, partnered by the new lad, but at least I wouldn't have to fetch the foreman's tea. From Monday that was the new lad's job – and he was welcome to it.

Then I realised that when the new lad came I wouldn't be the newest apprentice anymore. On Monday morning I would suddenly move up a rung on the Toolroom's social ladder, my present place as lowliest member of the pecking order being taken by the newcomer. And waiting in the wings for his nervous entrance was: a long stand; a perplexing mild steel toolbit that wouldn't cut anything; a large L plate hooked on to a collar, and the ongoing, vivid, all-embracing glory of the Engineer's Blue – I could hardly wait!

So we came to our last Friday before the move, and as we settled ourselves between the shapers at lunch-time a sudden shout of 'Gerroff!' echoed in from the Tool Repair. We scrambled to look through the arch to see Andy struggling furiously in the grip of two much larger figures. And even as we watched, our friend's wildly threshing form was lifted aloft and borne inexorably along the passageway towards the waiting wet grinder tank.

'Les Bonner and Jimmy Green,' announced Freddie. 'He's had it now!'

Even though there were three of us we made no attempt to aid our friend – nor would he have thanked us for any intervention. Initiation was a test which must be faced alone, and an apprentice's future status in the eyes of his workmates very much depended on how well he withstood that test. Without actually drawing blood – that was strictly taboo – the initiate was expected to put up a good fight before being overwhelmed and Andy was certainly doing that. Arms and legs, momentarily freed, lashed out in all directions. Les got a swipe on the back of his head that nearly took it off his shoulders, whilst Jimmy's grin was suddenly wiped away by a flailing elbow in the mouth.

We dashed along near the office, where we could get a better view of the climax of the struggle through another arch. Attracted by the noise, there was quite an audience to the show now, and shouts of encouragement for both camps rose excitedly.

'Upside down Jimmy – and keep 'im there for ten minutes!'

'Come on Andy!' roared the apprentices in opposition.

'Gerri's head in Les!' came a raucous shout.

Swiftly countered by Freddie's strident, 'Kick 'em in the bollocks Andy!'

Leaning against the doorpost of the Hardening Shop, the tall, boiler-suited figure of Les Jones, (known colloquially as the 'The Soft Hardener'), watched the battle dispassionately as he took large bites out of a door-step sandwich held in one grimy hand.

The struggling group finally reached the tank. To a chorus of cheers and boos Jimmy kicked the lid off. Andy was like an octopus with arms and legs appearing in all directions, fastening limpet-like on to parts of the wet grinder. They were all tiring now and try as they might, as we cheered ourselves hoarse, the initiators could not get the victim in the upside down position.

Then there was a loud splash. Grinning and panting heavily, Jimmy and Les stood back leaving Andy, with water swirling above his knees, standing in the tank. The battle was over. To prolonged applause the initiate wearily climbed out of the tank, shook his fist good humouredly at his assailants and sloshed his way into the Toolroom for his lunch.

'Well done!' we applauded as, still panting from his exertions, he sat down on a stool and began to unlace his shoes.

'That showed the bastards!' chortled Freddie. 'They didn't get your head in like they did with me!'

Andy grinned tiredly. 'I'm knackered – and soaked.' He took off his shoes and poured the water out. 'What am I going to do for the rest of the day? I can't stand around like this.'

I had a thought. 'Put your stuff by the furnaces, they'll dry in no time.'

'Good idea,' said the soaked initiate.

He spent the rest of lunch-hour sitting in the Hardener's in his underpants with trousers and socks dangling between the two big furnaces. They dried all right in the intense heat – they also shrank! Those trousers, once he had squeezed back into them, looked more like horse riding jodhpurs, ending a good two inches above his ankles and causing much amusement to all and sundry for the rest of the afternoon.

But Friday wasn't over and the grand finally was yet to come. We'd been paid and as knocking-off time approached, a deep, spasmodic thumping began to be heard above the noise of the machines. The sound originated from heavy lead, weights being dropped on the wooden benches, and it was the prelude to another long Meccano tradition – the great Toolroom Rally!

The object of the Rally was noise, and the louder the better. Anything was used. Hammers, copper mallets, lead weights and chunks of metal, bashed enthusiastically on benches and steel locker tops; whistling, cheering and stamping for those who had nothing to bash.

But before the deafening crescendo was reached, a certain procedure was followed. Like an orchestra tuning up, the random thuds of the big weights gradually merged into one deep bass 'Boom.' The bench light-shade tappers would join in then with the treble, a musical, metallic 'Ting.' So we had: Boom – Ting, Boom – Ting, Boom – Ting. The rest of us, the bashers, cheered and whistled, until the appropriate moment before unleashing our thunderous, discordant climax.

To some this noise-making was a serious business. Fred Dodd returned home from an Austrian holiday gleefully sporting a green William Tell hat and a small, bugle-like hunting horn which emitted a raucous, ear-splitting squeal, bought especially for Rally duty.

And what was the purpose of all this hooliganistic racket? Quite simple really. It was the Toolroom's noisy way of saying goodbye to someone who was leaving the fold for pastures new – only in this case it was airfields new, as the subject of the Rally was off to do his National Service in the RAF.

Tall, with black hair, Billy Hudson was well liked, so his Rally would be a good one. A leaver's popularity could be judged by the amount of noise that accompanied him through the door.

Billy had done the rounds of shaking hands and saying farewells and in return had received a little advice and an abundance of commiserations. Now we waited for him to walk out with his toolbox.

Boom –Ting; Boom – Ting; Boom – Ting.

'Hurry up Billy,' called a voice. 'The wife says my teas getting cold!'

Boom – Ting; Boom – Ting; Boom - Ting.

The machines were all stopped now. The shaper crew had their lead lumps poised expectantly above the steel lockers.

Boom – Ting; Boom – Ting; Boom – Ting.

In time to the rhythm a voice rose in song, the refrain quickly being taken up by more voices:

'So long it's been good to know ya,
So long it's been good to know ya,
So long it's been good to know ya . a . a . a,
It's two long years that you'll be gone ... so you'd better be drifting along.'

Boom – Ting; Boom – Ting; Boom – Ting.

Andy hurried up in his jodhpurs, seized a block of metal from my job and joined me poised over the locker top. He gave an exaggerated wink. 'It's more fun in here.'

The rhythm suddenly changed as a big weightier went out on his own.

Boom – Ting – Thud; Boom – Ting – Thud.

Billy lifted his box and began the long walk to the door. This was it!

Bang! Bang! Bang! Bang! We battered the living daylights out of our lockers.

Bang! Bang! Bang! He was turning the corner.

Bang! Bang! Bang! We were cheering now. The noise was indescribable. Blocks fell off the locker, just missing our feet, and still we bashed.

Bang! Bang! Bang! Bang! Bang! Bang! Whistling, cheering shouting and yelling we Rallied the new RAF recruit's final wave through the door and halfway down the corridor.

As the noise died away the Rally's final shout echoed across the silent machines, leaving a ripple of laughter. 'And if he decides to bomb the place from his aeroplane, I hope he starts with the office!'

Flushed with excitement I picked up the fallen lumps of metal, eyeing Andy's strait-jacketed legs. 'Your mum's going to kill you when she sees those trousers.'

He shrugged. 'They're an old pair, she won't be bothered. It was a good Rally wasn't it?'

'It sure was,' I agreed. 'My ears are still ringing.'

Chris came over. 'What a racket! I think I've gone deaf.'

'That's playing with yourself,' observed Andy. 'It makes you go deaf.'

'You should know,' grinned his friend. 'Which mob are you going in for your Nat. Service?'

Andy snorted. 'None! I'm not bloody well going ... '

'Nor me,' I chimed in.

'Anyway,' continued Andy, 'it makes no odds, it'll be finished by the time we're twenty one.'

'So you hope,' remarked Chris.

So we all hoped and we were all going to be disappointed. Voicing our thoughts on Monday's new apprentice we washed our hands and went home.

It was chucking it down on Monday morning and as I watched the foreman walk briskly back to his office, I wriggled my toes in a vain attempt to find a dry spot in my sodden socks. Cycling, even on a Claude Butler, lost much of its appeal under a flapping. sweaty cape with the rain trickling in your shoes.

Chris stopped his shaper and came down the passage. 'The new lad's just arrived,' he said as he passed. 'Sinbad's just told me to go and collect him.'

*

Chips of metal pinged against the guard as the toolbit progressed steadily across the square of steel. It was all so familiar now, and a far cry from that first, nervous entrance all those months ago. Meccano had brought me a long way since then. I wondered how the new lad was feeling, waiting in that narrow, unfriendly room; pretty nervous too, I'd bet. Well he'd soon get over that once he'd met us lads and realised that there was nothing to worry about.

Nervous? Worried? If such words had ever entered the new apprentice's vocabulary it had only been a fleeting visit. Radiating confidence, with a dazed looking Chris in tow, the new lad strode into the Toolroom like an embryonic managing director come to survey his future kingdom. From his black, Brylcreemed hair to his highly polished shoes he was impressive – and he knew it!

Chris was in desperate need of an ally. 'This is Basil,' he said hurriedly as they reached the shapers. 'And this is Roy.'

He was taller than me and his handshake was firm and confident. 'Glad to meet you Bas.' I said cheerfully, and was immediately corrected.

'Basil, if you don't mind,' he said shortly.

So that's the way it was, was it? Well, we'd see about that!

As my machine took some time to traverse across the large piece of die-cast tool, I was able to observe Basil's efforts to teach Chris how to operate the shaper. The only trouble was that Chris seemed to be under the impression that it was his job to teach Basil. It was all very entertaining and time passed quickly, until suddenly it was time to go for the foreman's tea. No it wasn't! If I waited a little while I could treat the new apprentice to the delightful experience of being caught in the Rush.

I timed it to the minute before I stopped my machine. 'Hey Basil!' He came over. 'It's time to go for Sinbad's tea.'

I was fixed with a questioning look. 'Sinbad?'

'The foreman – Jack Simpson.'

'What's all this about?'

Quite clearly Chris hadn't plucked up enough courage to tell him.

'Come on!' I urged. 'I'll explain as we go. We're late, and Sinbad will hit the roof if his tea's late and you'll get a right bollocking.'

That little speech stopped the questions and we hurried through the door to wash our hands.

Basil didn't like carrying that tray one little bit, but he had no choice. Until the next apprentice came he was stuck with providing the foreman's tea twice a day and I couldn't help rubbing it in a little.

'I'm glad you've come,' I said cheerfully, as we descended the canteen steps. 'It's bloody awful being the tea-lad, I've been sick to death of it for months. Still, it's your job now so I'm out of it – and bloody good riddance!'

Basil glared down at the loaded tray. 'It's bloody stupid,' he said bitterly. 'I don't see what this has to do with learning to be a toolmaker..'

I happily agreed with him. 'Neither do I, but that's the way of things at Meccano. We apprentices have to do as we're told – or else!'

Right on time the hooter shattered the pre tea-break calm as we were directly beneath it. Disappointingly the tray carrier's only reaction was a brief glance upwards.

We passed the cloak room cages and neared the corner. The sound of the Rush was rapidly growing louder, and not wishing to intrude upon my new friend's first encounter with the Meccano girls, I hung back a little. Round the corner strode unsuspecting Basil, the tray held out stiffly in front of him – straight into the path of the tightly packed female juggernaut. To give him credit he stood his ground – or was it shock! For a moment I was tempted to leave him to his fate, but I couldn't do it.

'Get back round the corner you fool!' I cried. 'They'll flatten you!'

And without a second bidding he got – and got with frantic speed!

Waiting for the flood to subside I noted, with a certain satisfaction, the pale face, strands of hair hanging loosely down and the gentle rattling crockery on the foreman's tray. The first lesson had been a definite success.

But the success was to prove short-lived. Basil soon recovered from his fright and spent most of the tea-break telling us of his future plans, and how his apprenticeship was only a stepping-stone to greater things. Concerted efforts to stem the flow were to no avail, and by the time the welcome hooter signalled the end of our break, we were all thoroughly fed-up and the new lad was miles ahead on points.

The rain had stopped so we took our lunch-time stroll up Binns Road. 'It's bloody awful!' exclaimed Chris. 'He's such a bloody know-all. Every time I try to show him something he'll say –'Yes I know,' or 'Simple, isn't it?' 'He's driving me round the bloody bend!'

'Kick him in the balls!' advised Freddie. 'That'll shut him up!'

'No it wouldn't,' Chris said gloomily. 'He'd probably tell me I'd done it the wrong way – the bloody smart-arse!'

It was quite obvious that the present state of affairs could not be allowed to continue. After all, a new lad was at the very bottom of the heap and had to know his place, and if he didn't know already then it was our duty to point him firmly in the right direction. Having decided on a solution, we took ourselves to the nearby park where we could swing on the maypole and formulate our plans.

And so:

Monday. The afternoon passed without incident. Basil went home in high spirits; Chris on the verge of a nervous breakdown.

Tuesday. Basil spent most of the day wearing a large L plate hooked on to his collar. Chris 'discovered' the notice just before clocking-off time and presented it to the victim. Basil went off home rather subdued, no doubt realising why chuckles and giggles had followed him round all day.

Wednesday. Basil went home sporting a beautiful blue eye from the afternoon tea-break.

Thursday. Basil rather quiet and paying closer attention to Chris's teaching. He went to the Tool Stores for a long stand and came back rather subdued again.

Friday. In the late afternoon, Basil mysteriously covered himself in Engineer's Blue when he was cleaning and oiling the shaper, under Chris's supervision.

All the lads went home feeling rather pleased with the weeks work.

On Monday morning Basil seemed to have become Bas over the weekend, who seems a rather likeable bloke and much easier to get on with.

A few weeks later Jimmy Green left. The un-initiated apprentices Rallied him out enthusiastically and heaved sighs of relief. Although we liked Jimmy – he rode an AJS trials motorbike, which impressed us no end – he was one of the wet grinder tank's most ardent devotees and never missed an opportunity to dump some unsuspecting young lad into that murky water.

Jimmy had gone, but Johno remained, so we still had to be on our guard.

Dark haired and handsome Ronnie Johnson was the heart-throb of many a Meccano girl – and the bane of many apprentices. He'd recently completed his National Service in the RAF and, on his return, lost no time in showing the youngest members of the Toolroom that they'd better watch out when he was around – or else!

But Johno also had another side to his nature – he was a showman. He enjoyed being in the limelight, a trait which often gave rise to the most outrages, and at times positively dangerous, practical jokes, particularly when he was aided and abetted by another lover of practical jokes, Tony Smith, or Smithy as he was usually called. We laughed heartily at the results of many of these escapades, but from a distance, and the further away the better!

Chris was in the Tool Repair now and Andy was back in the Toolroom on the small Dekel miller. Bas and I got along together but I was getting bored with the shaper and looked forward to moving on to learn the skills of cutter grinding. Then one warm, spring morning, an event occurred which relieved any boredom and in a most unexpected and startling fashion.

The Case of the Missing Underwear

Bas was off with the flu (the flu in spring?), so I reverted to tea-lad. As I came down the Canteen steps a girl was walking along the passage ahead of me. I didn't see her face but she was obviously young with blond hair and wearing a very short green overall. She began to ascend the steps of the cast iron fire escape to the Model Room, which was often used as a short cut to the Canteen., and as I passed I raised my eyes for a surreptitious look at those shapely legs.

My guardian angel must have had a tight grip on Sinbad's tray that morning because I promptly forgot all about it at the totally unexpected sight that met my astonished eyes through the open ironwork of the steps. I saw those shapely legs alright, but I also saw a pair of even more shapely, rounded buttocks and everything else I wasn't supposed to see – because that blonde-haired girl was going around without wearing any underwear.

My mouth must have dropped open as I feasted my eyes on the forbidden view. Transfixed, I stood as the buttocks' owner slowly ascended the steps - and nearly died of shock when a voice whispered in my ear: 'And what are you up to, standin' there with your mouth open – catchin' flies?'

Peeping Tom caught in the act!

Scarlet faced I whipped round. Frank the welder, welding mask in one hand, managed to save Sinbad's tea and toast with the other.

'I . I . I . I...' I stammered, hurriedly straightening the tray and even more hurriedly trying to think up an explanation for my intense fire escape gazing. I was looking at the fire escape steps and wondering how they cast them!' I blurted out.

Frank chuckled as a door clicked shut above our heads. 'And are you any wiser now you've had a good look?'

He knew! He bloody well knew and he was toying with me. I didn't want to gain a reputation as the dirty little bugger who sneaked about looking up unsuspecting girls skirts.

Hoping he wouldn't spread the story around I kept up the charade. 'Not really. I'll ask one of the toolmakers, it would be interesting to find out how it's done.'

Frank chuckled again, swinging the mask carelessly. 'I thought all you Toolroom lads already knew how it was done.'

'I'd better go,' I said hastily. 'Sinbad will be wondering why his tea's late.'

A laughing: 'Well I wouldn't tell 'im if I were you – he'd never believe it!' echoed after me along the passage.

With my friend, of course, it was different. We'd hardly sat down before I was gloatingly pouring the story into their envious, and at first disbelieving ears.

'No knickers!' cried Andy. 'Girls don't go round without their knickers, it would be too draughty for one thing!'

'A Model Room girl does,' I said smugly. 'Cos I've seen her naked bum – and it was lovely.'

'Cor!' breathed Freddie. 'You lucky devil! Was she a real blonde?'

'You can't tell,' said Chris knowledgeably. 'Real blondes have dark pubes the same as brunettes. The only ones who are different are red heads.'

Andy stared at him. 'How do you know?'

Chris wagged a finger. 'Aha. That would be telling wouldn't it.'

'Well I'd like to find out for myself,' drooled Freddie, and added wistfully. 'I wish I was getting Sinbad's tea.'

For weeks after the incident the Model Room fire escape was rarely without a hopeful apprentice lurking nearby, but the girl was never seen again. In desperation, Freddie made an illicit sortie into the Model Room to at least set eyes on the knicker-less goddess. He came back with a bollocking and the information that no young blonde was currently working there. Reluctantly we came to the conclusion that the girl had left, dyed her hair a different colour or caught pneumonia through going around half naked, which was a pity really; I would have so liked to have known if the rest of her was even half as attractive as that beautiful, unforgettable derriere.

*

Meccano's apprentice intake was accelerating. Only a few months after Basil's entrance, quiet, solemn Gerry appeared to take over my shaper. He did so awash with Engineer's Blue and trailing an endless procession of L plates. He was even persuaded to ask for a sky hook to go with the long stand. Basil was getting some of his own back.

I went up another rung on the ladder and was poised to take up residence in the very lair of the dreaded wet grinder tank. Chris had managed to escape an immersion – I hoped I would be as lucky.

I bumped into Johno at the wash basins. 'I see you've got a new lad,' he said in his sneering voice.

'Yeh.' I answered, poising myself for a quick getaway – you never knew with Johno. 'His name's Gerry, he seems okay.'

He pulled the roller towel round, seeking a dry part and giving vent to an irritable: 'Bloody hell! These towels are always bloody soaking!'

I edged away. An irritable Johno was even more unpredictable.

He looked down at me, mouth curved sardonically. 'So you'll be in the Tool Repair soon?'

I edged further away. 'Yeh. probably on Monday.'

'We'll get you then,' he taunted. 'Head first in the wet grinder tank.'

'You'll have a bloody good try!' I retorted – and fled.

They didn't get me; in fact they never even tried. When Jimmy Green left most of the enthusiasm for the initiation ceremony went with him – as is often the way. But we apprentices were not to know this, and the dripping spectre of the wet grinder tank continued to hover over our working lives as real and menacing as ever.

So, uninitiated, I learnt the art of cutter grinding – for it is an art. Achieving the correct angle for a sharp and lasting edge on metal cutting tools was no easy task. I took great delight in fitting useless, blunt and chipped milling cutters to the small cutter grinder and seeing them, after much painstaking work, glittering and razor sharp again.

Sometimes I would go down to the Machine Shop, where all the gears were cut, or into the Toolroom, and take great delight in watching my revitalised cutters effortlessly carving their way through the metal.

And that training, as with most of my learning at Meccano, has stood me in good stead down the years; for in that smoke-grimed factory on Binns Road we were taught an engineering excellence which was known and respected all over the world.

Summer holidays arrived and, as with Christmas, there was a festive air about the place. The final pay-day was indeed bountiful for besides the golden eagle's normal egg, everyone received a double-yolk in the form of two week's holiday pay.

I hadn't been there for long enough so I only got an extra yoke and a half, which was one and a half times more than our newest recruit, Gerry. He didn't even get the shell!

We cleaned and oiled our machines, smearing oil on all the bare metal surfaces so they didn't rust during the shut-down; swapped holiday destinations and left the toys and trains and Meccano sets for the sun, sand and sea.

Disaster! Andy and I had gone Youth Hostelling in North Wales on our bikes – my first holiday away from my parents. Three days out, at Llanrwst, I caught an extremely virulent dose of flue (the flue in summer?), and we had to come home on the train from Betws-y-Coed, bikes and all. Weak as a kitten and aching all over, I spent the rest of my holiday languishing in bed at my Auntie Molly's as my mum and dad, along with thousands of other lucky Liverpudlians, were whooping it up in the Isle of Man.

So we returned to the silent, oil glistening machines. Most of the workers were glistening too, with suntan oil on their sunburnt faces. I was as pale as a ghost and a stone lighter.

A few months later Gordon arrived and it was all change again for the apprentice population.

In many respects I was sorry to move. I enjoyed cutter grinding and even the wet grinder, which I also operated, had its moments, and the atmosphere in the Tool Repair was far more relaxed than the main Toolroom. This was mainly due to the foreman, Bill Jackson, a big, bluff man who held the reigns of his department with a competent but easy hand.

Of Trusses & the Single Testicle

I hadn't been back in the Toolroom for long when the 'Incident' with the slotter operator occurred. During the shut down some of the machines had been moved and Fred's slotter was now on the opposite side of the passage, near the band-saw. I was now operating the Dekel miller, bench lathe and band-saw, and had been to the office for a requisition, but Sinbad was out, and as I came back along the passage Fred was bending over the slotter table, with the machine stopped, scrutinising the job. He was a rather skinny individual and the flaps of his work coat had fallen open, exposing a hanging pouch of trouser seat. To this day I don't know what possessed me to do it – but do it I did. As I passed I grabbed that so-inviting pouch and whipped it smartly in an upwards direction.

Either Doddy was lighter than he looked, or I was stronger than I realised – either way the result was the same. As I gave my frivolous heave, the slotter operator shot up in the air like a rocket and almost did a somersault over the top of his machine. I don't know who was the most surprised, but as Doddy descended to earth again, in a flurry of wildly kicking legs, I was definitely the more shocked.

Instantly I realised the enormity of what I had done as, face aflame, nose purple with rage, my victim rounded on me.

'You stupid little bugger!' he yelled. 'What the bloody hell are you playing at! I wear a bloody truss – you could have done me a real injury!.'

As Fred's face was red, mine must have been chalk white.

'S.s.sorry Fred,' I stammered. 'I didn't realise that would happen.'

Glowering at me he smoothed his overall down. 'You bloody idiot! You should be locked up! Keep your bloody hands to yourself in future or you'll be straight into the office!'

I grinned ingratiatingly. 'Sorry Fred,' I repeated. 'I'll never do it again – honestly.'

'You'd better bloody not!' he snorted. 'Now bugger off and get on with your work!'

I buggered off – smartly.

At lunch-time I asked the company in general, 'What's a truss?'

Chris shrugged, 'I dunno.'

Andy looked equally blank.

Freddie provided the answer. 'It's like a brassiere, only instead of keeping tits up it holds your balls in place.'

This was news. 'Why?' I asked.

'Stops your knees banging against them,' declared our informant knowledgeably.

'But my knees don't bang against mine.'

He grinned. 'They will as you get older, your bag stretches with the weight, then you'll have to wear a truss – see!'

We roared derisively at the very thought, but in the absence of more expert enlightenment, we had to be content with the inverted brassiere explanation.

And hot on the heels of the truss came the story of the single testicle!

A rumour began to circulate that one of the toolmakers had to go for an operation because only one of his balls had dropped. Dropped! Dropped where? This news flash caused a big ripple in the male pond, particularly amongst the younger members who were rather ignorant as far as technical testicle information was concerned. We all had two, and Freddie had told us about the truss that could be used if your bag ever stretched. Other than that what could possibly go wrong?

The news caused a bit of a traffic jam at the toilets as close, self examination was undertaken by both young, and not so young engineers, to reassure themselves that everything was in its place and as it should be. Nobody seemed to know who the unfortunate victim was and even wide-spread scrutinising of the way people walked shed no light. We all heaved a sigh of relief when a better informed individual came up with the explanation. The problem only came to light when the person wanted to start a family, otherwise there was nothing to worry about.

The news did however give rise to the memory, and singing of the derisory, war-time song about Adolf Hitler and his gang of thugs either having only one testicle or none at all.

Sung to the tune of Colonel Bogey, this ditty rapidly became 'top of the pops' for all the budding singers in the Toolroom.

Cupid, Draw Back Your Bow

I was in love. Passionately! Deliriously! Head over heels in love. I had disturbed sleep; was off my food; and my working day was only made bearable by hoping for an occasional glimpses of the green-overalled goddess who was the cause of all my misery.

Cupid had twanged his bow and scored a direct hit one morning as I waited in the queue at the Toolroom tea-trolley. The tea lady was busy filling mugs from the urn and dispensing greasy, hot toast and even greasier sausage rolls. The younger members of the queue were equally busy, dispensing lecherous remarks concerning the hundreds of females who were crowding past the Toolroom windows.

'There's Big Tits,' said Chris, who was in front of me. 'I'm going to ask her out one of these days and find out if they're real.'

'Falsies!' stated Andy. 'You can tell that a mile away. Nobody's built like that. I'll bet she's got a couple of pounds of cotton wool stuffed down there.'

Chris gazed at the subject of the discussion. 'Well I think you're wrong. They wouldn't wobble like that if they were falsies. I wouldn't mind finding out, and just imagine if they were real. Wow! He nudged me with his elbow. 'What do you think Roy? Falsies or real?'

But I hardly heard him. All my attention was focused on an elfin face, surrounded by a halo of dark hair that was just passing the Toolroom doorway. It was only a glimpse in the sea of faces and then she was gone, but that brief glimpse set my pulse racing. 'Wow!' I breathed.

Chris nudged me again. 'Well?'

I came back to earth. 'Well what?'

'Good grief! Have you gone deaf? You want to stop playing with it. I was talking about Big Tits, are they real or falsies?'

'Not interested in scrubbers,' I said loftily, as we shuffled nearer the trolley. 'I've just seen a little cracker.'

Eyes swivelled towards the windows, scanning the faces.

Andy frowned. 'Where is she? I don't see anything special.'

To late I realised my mistake in telling. I knew only too well that when attractive girls came on the scene, friendship went straight out of the window and it was every man for himself. I tried to undo the damage. 'Oh she's gone now. I only saw her face anyway. She's probably a scrubber and bandy with no tits.' An explanation that fooled no-one.

'Oh no you don't,' Chris said as we shuffled forward again. 'He's spotted something special, hasn't he Andy? And now he's trying to put us off the scent.'

'It would certainly appear that way,' came the solemn reply. 'Attempting to hide the crumpet from one's mates is not a nice thing to do – not nice at all. I'm thinking we shall have to keep a close eye on our young friend.'

'We certainly shall,' agreed Chris. 'A very close eye indeed.'

Since the last move round we had changed our tea-break base to near the horizontal miller, which Chris was operating, leaving between the shapers to Bas, Gerry and Gordon. So tea'd and sausage-rolled we settled down with Freddie, our tea-break companion, and the inquisition began.

'Roy's just spotted a new bit of crumpet,' Andy informed Freddie.

'Oh aye. What's she like?' asked Freddie, with great interest. 'Is she worth poking?'

'Well might you ask,' sniggered Chris. 'Cos he's not talking.'

'Oh come on,' I protested. 'I only caught a glimpse of her. She probably won't be up to much when you see her properly.'

'Ha!' jeered Chris. 'Just listen to him. You should have seen him, Freddie, when he spotted her, drooling and buckling at the knees he was. He didn't even give Big Tits a second look, he was so excited!'

'What a load of— ' I began but Freddie interrupted.

'Big Tits? Where was she? I didn't see her.' He leered, puffing his cheeks out. 'Now there's a girl I'd like to be locked in a bedroom with!'

'That's a laugh!' jeered Andy, taking a bite of his roll. 'You wouldn't know what to do – you're all talk.' He made a face. 'Yuk! This sausage roll's bloody awful! I think they're making them with old cutting oil.'

'Who wouldn't know what to do?' retorted Freddie, with spirit. 'You just fix me up and I'll show her a thing or two I can tell you!'

'Got more than one have you?' asked Chris interestedly.

Freddie grinned. 'Wouldn't you like to know.'

Andy snorted derisively. 'I don't know what you're bragging about, you're too scared to even ask her for a date. Like I said – you're all talk!'

Freddie flushed. 'Well we'll see. You might be in for a surprise one day soon. Then we'll see who's all talk.' He took a gulp of tea and leaned back against the miller, smirking at our baffled expressions.

'Well go on,' I said. 'Who are you fixed up with?'

He looked at us smugly. 'Oh no you don't. I'm saying nothing. But,' he added darkly, 'I'll tell you one thing – you'll all be dead jealous.'

There was a silence as we all chewed on our sausage rolls

and wondered who Eddie was talking about and if he really did have a date.

Then Chris said, 'Did she have blonde hair, Roy?'

'No black,' I answered absently.

There was a shout of laughter!

'So your mysterious bird has black, does she?' grinned Andy. 'Well done Chris.'

His friend bowed his head modestly. 'All in the line of duty you know, Andy.'

Freddie smirked at me. 'Black hair eh? Now there's a coincidence.'

My heart sank. Could it be possible that Freddie – scruffy Freddie – of all people had pipped me to the post! No! It was unthinkable. As far as we knew, Freddie had never had a date in his life, as Andy had said he was all talk. But doubt persisted, what had he meant by black hair being a coincidence?

'Short, black hair,' said Freddie, grinning at my startled expression.

'Dead wrong!' I retorted. 'It was long if you must know. So bugger off!'

With the air of a detective who has just discovered a vital clue Andy raised his eyebrows. 'Definitely short, black hair,' he stated blandly.

'Definitely!' chorused the other two.

I was losing hands down, and losing my temper into the bargain – fatal in this situation. Unable to think of a suitable sarcastic retort, I ignored further taunting and kept a stony silence until the long, drawn-out wail of the hooter signalled the end of the break, and the end of the inquisition – for the moment.

We drifted back to our machines. The factory began to hum again as electric motors and machinery started up.

The small Dekel miller I was operating, slitting small, spray holders for the Dinky Toy spray lines, was near the windows of the main corridor. As I worked, leaning against a large cupboard, I had a good view of the corridor and the entrance to the female toilets at the end of the Press Shop. If I kept a watchful eye open, I might be lucky enough to get a good look at the girl if she came down, and with a bit more luck I might be able to follow her back, find out where she worked and half my problems would be over.

Such were my thought as I turned the handles, sending the whirring, cutter slicing into the metal. It was a monotonous job making these spray holders. Small, narrow rods, a couple of inches long, had to have a small shoulder turned on one end and a hole drilled up the other on the bench lathe. The shouldered part was slit through in a cross to enable it to contract and grip in a recess cast in the body of the Dinky Toy, usually the inside of the roof. Hundreds of rods were mounted on a slow-moving conveyer, so the toys could be sprayed, and then passed through an oven so the paint was dry when they came out the other end.

Whether some enterprising worker in the Spray Shop had another use for those small rods I never discovered, but the demand for them was never ending.

With a loud, musical twang, a piece suddenly broke out of the saw, a regular occurrence if you weren't paying attention as the cutter was extremely hard high speed steel and very thin. After a good root through the cupboard failed to reveal any cutters of the right thickness, I set off for the office for a requisition. I had a sneaking suspicion that my request would not be well received by my foreman, and I was right!

'Come in!' was the terse response to my tentative knock.

I climbed the two steps and opened the door. Sinbad was

sitting at his desk. He looked up, his glasses two small mirrors in the fluorescent light.

'Yes?'

'Er, could I have a requisition for some cutters, please?'

He frowned, then deliberately put down his pen. 'We seem to be having a rather high mortality rate on these cutters, Byrne. Have you any idea why?'

From the tone of his voice I knew I was in for a bollocking. I swallowed, 'Er. No.'

The glasses glinted like razors. 'No? Well in that case I'd better enlighten you.' He smiled coldly. 'In my experience frequent tool breakage is almost always caused by careless-ness. In your case your interest appears to focus more on the females walking up and down outside than it does on your work. I want to see that state of affairs reversed. Understood?'

I swallowed again. 'Yes sir.'

He reached for the requisition pad. 'Good! Now what size are those cutters?'

At the Tool Stores I sought an ally against authority. 'I've just had a right bollocking off that bastard Sinbad!' I ranted to Mike as I handed him the requisition. 'He said I broke cutters because I was piping the girls in the passage instead of concen-trating on the job.'

He grinned. 'I'll bet he's right too.'

'Of course he's right!' I retorted, 'But if he was doing that lousy job I'll bet he'd be eyeing the talent as well – bloody spray holders!'

Mike leaned over the counter. 'The thing is, you have to play it crafty and not make it so obvious. What I do is— '

He was interrupted by a voice behind him. 'It's obvious that someone else is going to get a rocket as well if he doesn't get on with his work instead of talking.'

Mike raised his eyes to heaven and hurried away.

Holding his glasses up on his forehead, Bill Cherry was looking at me from behind his desk. 'You're all the same you apprentices,' he said severely. 'You mess about and when you get told off you come down here moaning and stopping my lads from working. Serves you right I say.'

I was in no mood for lectures. 'Oh come off it Bill. You lot in here hardly have anything to do anyway, so how can we stop you working?'

The florid face deepened in colour. 'What! Nothing to do!' he spluttered. 'I'll have you know that we work jolly hard in here – and stop being cheeky!' The glasses snapped down and he went back to his books.

Mike returned and winked as he handed me the cutters. 'There you go, and less of the bird watching.'

The rest of the morning passed uneventfully, with no more broken cutters and, despite a sharp look-out on my part, no further sightings of the dark-haired beauty.

Lunch-time came with the usual blast of sound from the hooter. The busy hum of machinery dwindled and died away, leaving that almost unnatural stillness which always seems to fill an idle factory. Different sounds began to arise. Voices calling to friends. Stools and chairs being dragged across the floor to lunch-time corners; cups clinked and tin mugs clanked.

I went through the door and was swept down the corridor by the smoking, chattering female tide hurrying along on its way home or to the canteen.

The toilet door provided me with an escape and I slipped through to join a tightly packed, smoking, gossiping crowd of men. Pushing my way into a space I stood at the long urinal trough, idly listening to snatches of conversation floating above the general noise.

'That gear cutter's been a sod this morning ...' 'No sooner had I ...' 'Hey Alf! If you're going to the shops ...' 'Bloody hell it's crowded in here ...'

Someone pushed in beside me. 'That's a tiny thing you're holding,' said Freddie's voice in my ear.

'Your girlfriend likes it,' I retorted, giving the stock answer. 'Oh, I forgot. You haven't got one – *or* a girl friend.'

'I might have soon,' he grinned.

We pushed our way to the wash basins. 'I've been doing some silver soldering this morning,' Freddie informed me as we waited for the bowl to fill. 'It's a doddle.'

'I've been getting a bollocking off Sinbad,' I said gloomily. 'He said I'm breaking cutters because I'm eyeing up the talent and not watching what I'm doing.'

'Bloody hell!' he said. 'You want to watch it. Sinbad can make your life a misery if you get on the wrong side of him.'

I pulled the plug out. 'I know. I'm going to try and keep my nose clean for a bit. Are you coming to the shops?'

Before he had a chance to answer, we were jostled away from the basins by the men waiting behind us.

'Bloody Toolroom wallers,' growled a voice. 'Think they own the place.'

There could only be one response to such an insult and we responded. 'Get stuffed!' we chorused, and hurriedly made for the door to avoid any possible retribution.

Our hasty exit precipitated us into a group of girls who were passing, and in the confusion of bodies, I found myself looking at an elfin face surrounded by a halo of raven hair. It was the girl I had glimpsed that morning when I was waiting in the tea queue – and she was beautiful.

'S... sorry,' I stammered, as she stepped past me. She made no reply but a small, thin-faced girl, curlured hair covered by an orange, chiffon scarf, determined to make a fuss.

'Yous wanna luk were yer goin!' she shrilled, narrow features working with self-righteous indignation. 'Ya cud av 'urt one of us gerls, jumpin' out like dat! Ya paira ejits!'

At any other time I would have retaliated to this tirade from my growing store of sarcastic remarks, but that brief look into those dark, eyes had left me speechless and at the mercy of this sharp-tongued harpy.

Freddie had no such handicap. 'Call yourself a girl,' he jeered. 'You look more like a walking ironmonger's with all them curlers!'

Aghast at this verbal shouting match in front of the black-haired beauty, I grabbed my friend's hand and tried to pull him away from the battle zone. 'Shurrup!' I hissed.

'What's wrong with you?' he exclaimed. 'She's a right scrubber that one, I've had a row with her before.'

I managed to put some distance between us, with furious, strident tones echoing along the corridor. 'Yer all de same yous Toolroom lot! Don't care fer no one! Well I'm gonna report yous dis time!'

Freddie stopped, drawing breath to hurl another insult back. 'Shurrup!' I repeated, urgently, trying to think of a reason for surrender. 'If she complains I'll be in dead trouble, I've already had one bollocking off Sinbad this morning!'

He shrugged. 'Okay, but I don't know what you're worrying about, no-one would take any notice of that old boot anyway.'

We continued on our way back to the Toolroom. Anxious to change the subject in case Freddie put two and two together and come up with a certain girl, I asked, 'Are you coming to the shops?'

'I sure am. I want to get a paper to see if Liverpool got the new centre forward they were after.'

Inwardly I hugged myself. During our recent fracas, the girl – or my girl – as I thought of her, had gone unnoticed by my sharp-eyed friend. Admittedly he'd been locked in a verbal battle at the time but even so, had she been the subject of his veiled tea-break allusions to a dark-haired girl, he couldn't have resisted telling me the details. So my secret was safe – for the moment.

'You look pleased with yourself,' remarked Andy as I pulled a stool into our corner.

I opened my lunch-box, lifted the top off a sandwich and groaned. 'Sardines again! I wish my mum would give me something different for a change.'

'They're good for you,' said Chris. 'Put lead in your pencil.' He offered his box. 'I'll swap you for a cheese.'

Andy tapped me with his foot. 'I said you were looking pleased with your little self.'

'Do I?' I asked innocently, taking a bite from my sandwich.

'Yes you bloody well do!' said the great detective. He looked at me narrowly. 'You're up to something.'

Freddie unconsciously saved me from further cross exam-ination. 'We've just had a right dust-up at the bog. Someone made a snide remark about Toolroom people and we told him to get stuffed then belted out into a bunch of girls as they were passing. One of them made a right fuss, A real scrubber she was, with a face like a ferret and half a ton of curlers. She threatened to report us 'cos,' his voice rose to a squawk in a very passable imitation of ferret-face. 'Ya cud av ert one of us gerls, jumpin' out like dat – ya paira ejits!' We all laughed. Freddie continued. 'So I told her she looked like a walking ironmonger's. Boy was she mad, like a wet hen!'

'Serves her right,' chuckled Chris, 'she asked for it! But I wish they'd get some better talent in this place, they all seem to be scrubbers these days.'

'That's because you don't know where to look,' I said, smugly. 'Are you coming up to the shops?'

Andy stood up and stretched. 'I'm not, I'm making a poker. You know how it is.'

We all knew how it was, we budding toolmakers. When promoted to the big, centre lathe, one of the first 'foreigners' (jobs not for the company) an apprentice made was a poker.

Diligently he would cut a few inches of thread on one end of a round steel rod. Then he would saw rough discs of aluminium, copper, brass, red and black fibre and anything else suitable he could lay his hands on. These discs were drilled and threaded and screwed on to rod. This colourful mixture was then carefully machined in the lathe to an exotic shape, and polished to a glittering finish. This was the handle. The other end, the fire poking part, was also threaded, then fitted with a larger piece of steel – usually hexagonal – which in turn was carved into another exotic shape and highly polished. The finished would then be smuggled out of the factory under a shirt or down a trouser leg and carried home in triumph.

And what was it that drove the embryonic turner to such dedication? Was it a desire to see the joy in his fond mother's eyes when she was finally presented with the fruits of his labour? Or perhaps it was a yearning to keep the home fires burning brightly? Sadly, there was no such selfless motives. The truth was that those precious lunch-hours were sacrificed on the demanding altar of tradition. In short, the apprentice made a poker because it was expected of him, and he knew no peace until the zealous keepers of that tradition had seen, studied, and pronounced judgement on his offering.

But even when duty had been done it was not the end of the matter. The poker maker's proud mum would exhibit his masterpiece to all her friends and relations, and before he knew where he was there would be orders lined up for Auntie Nelly, Cousin Kate, Mrs. Jones next door-but-one and heaven knows who else, and the hapless apprentice would have to find some other time to eat because, for the foreseeable future, his lunch-hours would be given over to making poker, after poker, after poker. To add too his plight, somewhere in between these unwelcome orders, he would have to find time to make his mum another less glorious poker because, when the beginning of all his problems had first landed on the hearth, his delighted parent had promptly thrown her old poker in the bin and now didn't have the heart to use 'something so beautiful to poke the dirty fire.

Brian had my sympathy – his penance was just beginning; mine was an impossible distance in the future.

Lunch-time was nearly over as we joined the small queue at the clock and as I pressed the pointer into six two nine. The hooter wailed and quiet Gerry came hurrying up to clock on. It was an opportunity too good to miss, so as he reached for the pointer I indulged in the well-known pastime of spinning the arm. This trick always raised the amiable hope that the wildly gyrating steel arm might give the potential clocker-on a rest from his labours by removing a finger or two. Gerry's reflexes were too quick for an amputation.

'You nearly had him there,' remarked Chris as we strolled up the passage, leaving flustered Gerry trying to catch the wildly spinning arm.

'It was a bit lousy,' I admitted, feeling a twinge of remorse. 'I might have hurt the poor bugger if he hadn't been so quick.'

'He's got good reflexes all right,' agreed Freddie, 'Better

than mine anyway. That bloody Johno got me like that one day – nearly took my bloody hand off!'

There was a short silence. We'd all had dealings with Johno at some time.

'We should get him, you know.' said Chris. 'Teach him a lesson.'

'Get him in the bog!' cried Freddie enthusiastically. 'Shove his head down the lav and pull the chain. That'd teach him to lay off us.'

'He'd only catch us when we were on our own,' I said, gloomily, 'and he's too big for me for a start.'

'Well we'll just have to wait for a bit,' observed Freddie as we turned into the Toolroom. 'Then we'll get him good!'

Ten minutes into the afternoon, the sudden appearance of Sinbad's white coat beside me instantly changed my relaxed cupboard leaning to bolt upright keen interest in the job.

He motioned towards the machine. 'Switch off for a minute.'

With a sense of foreboding I pressed the red button.

For a moment the foreman looked at me directly, as if making up his mind about something. It had to be that ferret-faced girl's complaint. In silence I waited for the blow to fall. Was it another bollocking, or even worse, the dreaded suspension!

'There are quite a few new Dinky Toys in the pipeline,' he began.

The tension drained out of me like water. It wasn't another bollocking.

' ... and there is so much work on the slotter that Fred won't be able to machine all the blanking dies for the bases in time. Do you think you could cut some of them out on the band-saw?'

I blinked. I had seen enough press tools being made to realise that what the foreman was asking would not be easy, to say the least. I knew that a pierce and blank die was inch thick HRS carbon steel, that it was difficult to cut and that much expensive work had already been done before the base shape was cut out. I also knew, from bitter experience, the difficulty of using the band-saw for precision work. Supposing I made a mistake and cocked it up? Sinbad was waiting and there could only be one answer.

'I can do it.' I replied with more confidence than I was feeling.

His face relaxed. 'Good lad. Leave these now and go and see Bob Brown, he will tell you what he wants.'

He walked away, leaving me in a lather of nervous apprehension and the recurring thought that refused to go away : 'What happens if I cock it up?' But I had no option now; in fact I never had any option in the first place. To have admitted to my foreman that I thought the job beyond my capabilities could have blighted my whole future. Still, he must think I could do it or he wouldn't have asked, so now it was up to me to prove him right.

I tidied the machine and had a quick look out of the window in case a certain girl happened to be walking past, but the passage was empty. Well, my romantic aspirations would have to wait for a while now, Sinbad's request had completely altered my feelings towards my job. In giving me this opportunity to prove my skill he'd transformed spray holder boredom into keen interest, and if I were to succeed there could be no room for outside distractions – at least in working hours. With mounting confidence and determination I went to see Bob.

Ten minutes later my new-found confidence had been knocked flat!

Bob was a nice fellow and an excellent toolmaker; he was also extremely fussy, and lost no time in letting me know that he was very doubtful if I was capable of doing such a technical job. For him there was no second best, it had to be right and right first time, and I was left in no doubt that he viewed Sinbad's scheme, and my part in it, with a very jaundiced eye indeed.

'He's been to see me about it,' he said, grimly. 'And I told him it wouldn't work. I've never heard of a die aperture being cut out on the bloody band-saw. It's not accurate enough for a start, and you're only a young lad for a finish. The whole thing's going to be a complete cock-up!'

Parrot-like I repeated the foreman's reasons for this change in practice, and I was sure I could do the job.

'Yes! Yes!' he said, testily. 'I know all that, and I know you'll do your best.' He sighed resignedly. 'I don't suppose there's any option. I can't do it myself, I'm too busy with other stuff.' He fixed me with a glittering eye. 'You'd better not cock it up and don't leave too much filing out that's all!'

'I wont Bob,' I assured him, confidently.

The die was about eight inches by ten and was to make the base for the Riley Saloon, and as I looked at Bob's beautiful, neat marking out, and he painstakingly explained how I most cut to the edge of the line, which was only three thousands of an inch wide, and if I cut into that line by even a small nick the whole die would be scrap. I toyed with the idea of going off sick, but I was sure I could do it, and proving it to myself was now even more important than proving it to Bob or Sinbad or anyone else. So I duly took the precious lump of steel from its nervous owner and made my way back to the band-saw.

The band-saw, as the name implies, was an endless saw blade which revolved around two cased-in wheels, one above the other. It was over six feet high and had a large, flat table to support the material being cut. A small adjustable pipe puffed the filings away. The blade, which had teeth on one edge, came in a large coil, the correct length being measured to a certain number of tiles on the floor. Fixed to the left-hand side of the machine was a fascinating little brazing tool to join the two ends of the blade. Although a comparatively simple procedure, a fair amount of skill was required to make a strong, lasting joint. If the join was poor the blade would snap with a loud bang, instantly prompting loud cheers of derision from all within earshot. In the certain knowledge that one of those gun-shot reports would at least bring the Riley die's owner hurrying over, or possibly precipitate him into an early grave, I threaded the blade through one of the large holes that George had already drilled inside the marked out section, for easier access, and joined that blade with all the care and skill I possessed.

Once I began, my apprehension quickly vanished with the intense concentration the job demanded, and apart from the occasional glimpse of a pair of nervous eyes through the surrounding machines, I was left severely alone. Only at clocking off time did George venture over to see if his worst fears had been realised and I was more than happy to show him that his worrying had been unnecessary – up to now!

A cool breeze was blowing as I freewheeled down Binns Road, scanning the pavements in the hope of seeing my heart-throb and nearly fell off my bike when I glimpsed her in the crowd – or, at least, I thought I saw her.

Andy drew alongside. 'Hiya. You're early.'

'Hiya. So are you.'

'Under-slept!' he rejoined. 'Isn't she bloody gorgeous! I could hardly sleep last night thinking about her. Wait 'till I tell the rest of the lads.'

I nearly fell off my bike again. My secret was out! And once Andy spilt the beans half the Toolroom would be asking her for a date and where would I be then?'

'Look Andy,' I said earnestly. 'I wouldn't crack on about it if I were you. There's no point in telling the lads, they all be asking her out – and anyway, I saw her first.'

He looked at me. 'What the bloody hell are you going on about? How could we ask her out? Have you gone off your trolley or something?'

I had a sudden feeling that our wires were crossed. 'Just a joke,' I said feebly.

'Bloody daft joke!' he retorted.

Stopping, we threaded our way through the mass of people to the bike racks. Andy pushed his front wheel into a slot, leant his elbow on the saddle, cupped his chin in his hand, and with a dreamy look drooled, 'Audrey Hepburn – I love you.'

Then it all became clear. The previous evening Andy, Chris and I had been to the Curzon cinema to see *Roman Holiday*, with Audrey Hepburn as a princess who escapes from her court and spends the day incognito going round Rome with a journalist, played by Gregory Peck. We had all been in love with the beautiful actress as we left the cinema but by the time I jumped on the bus for home, my affections were already returning to my real-life princess. Reassured, I whistled happily as we went to clock on.

After a whole night in which to brood and worry, Bob was in no mood to leave me unsupervised for a second day. Every twenty minutes or so I would become aware of a slow, rhythmic breathing in my ear. 'Just wondered how it was going,' Bob would mutter as I looked round, and after an anxious peer at the die he'd wander back to his bench. It was very wearing and

I was glad when the hooter sounded for tea-break.

'That bloody Bob as driving me nuts,' I grumbled to Andy as we stood in the tea queue. 'He's round all the time, puffing his fag in my ear, to make sure I'm not cutting his precious die in half! I'm bound to mess it up if he keeps on.'

He chuckled. 'Bust the blade – that'll panic him.'

'It would panic me too; honestly he's really getting me down.'

'Tell him to bugger off then,' he suggested amiably. 'Anyway, that's your problem, I'm still in love with Audrey Hepburn.' He gave a long sigh. 'If only I could find a girl like her, I'd happily give up my wicked ways.'

'Ho! Ho!' I jeered. 'I'll believe that when it happens. It'd take more than Audrey Hepburn to make you … ' A casual glance through the doorway stopped me short, There she was! Standing in the passage not twenty feet away, laughing with a crowd of girls.

Andy followed my gaze. 'What's up? Oh is that the bird you were going on about? That black haired one?'

There was no point in lying, it would only make matters worse, so I confessed. 'Yeh it is. What do you think?'

He eyed the vision appraisingly before giving his verdict. 'Not bad I suppose.'

I could hardly believe my ears. Not bad! Not bad! Was he blind or something? Couldn't he see that even Audrey Hepburn couldn't hold a candle to this laughing beauty? I leapt to my beloved's defence. 'What do you mean – not bad? She's bloody lovely! She knocks scrawny Audrey Hepburn right out the window!'

There was a derisive laugh. 'You must be joking. She's prob- ably a scrubber anyway.'

I wasn't having that! 'She is not!' I said hotly. 'No-one so gorgeous could be a scrubber – so don't come that!'

'We'll soon find out,' he said, and leaning out of the queue he called, 'Hey Ronnie!'

'And I thought you were my friend,' I said, bitterly.

'I am,' he replied. 'Just proving a point that's all. He'll know if she's a scrubber, he seems to know every girl in the bloody factory.'

Johno sauntered up from the head of the queue, A brimming mug in his hand. despite the situation I couldn't help envying his dark, good looks.

'What?' he asked, insolently.

'That bird by the door,' said Andy. 'The one with black hair. Do you know her? Is she a scrubber?'

Johno stared. I thought of ways of murdering my friend.

The verdict came. 'A scrubber? She's not bad I suppose. Her name's Beverly; she works in the Train Room. The last time I was up there she was putting the wheels on Dinky toys. Why do you want to know?'

'Roy fancies her.'

Johno winked and knocked me with his elbow. 'You should be alright there. Wouldn't mind myself only she's a bit young for me.' He strolled away, leaving a trail of slopped tea from his over-filled mug.

'You bloody rat!' I exclaimed, viciously. 'I could bloody well strangle you, telling him about her!'

He grinned. 'I don't know what you're complaining about, at least you know her name now, and where she works.'

That was right of course. 'Well, keep your big mouth shut in future if you don't mind.' I said feebly.

He grinned again and handed his mug to the tea lady. 'Sugar and a sausage roll please, and a cuddle in the corner.'

The Beverly Botchup

I finished Bob's die and took it over to him. With his watchmaker's eyeglass he carefully scrutinised the aperture for what seemed like an eternity. Then, with a long exhalation of breath, he put the die down and clapped me on the shoulder. 'Good lad. Thanks a lot, I couldn't have done it better myself!'

Praise indeed.

I walked on air to the office, and rapped smartly on the door.

'Come in.'

'I've finished Bob's die,' I said confidently.

He looked up. 'And is it alright?'

This was my moment of glory. 'He said he couldn't have done it better himself.'

The thin lips twitched. 'Good lad, we'll make a toolmaker of you yet. Now go and see Jim Tullo, he has another die for you to do.'

If I'd walked on air into the office – I floated out on a rosy cloud. Life was looking good. I'd beautiful completed a difficult job and done it well. I was firmly in Tiggy's good books – for a change – and not only did I know where my girl worked, I also knew her name as well. Beverly. What a name for such a beautiful girl. Much more appropriate than Mary, Teresa or dismal Edna. Beverly, Beverly, Beverly, whispered in my mind, sounding sweeter with every step I took to my next job.

I liked Jim. Small and muscular with slicked down, brown

hair, he sported a thin, neat moustache and had a ready sense of humour. You could always be sure of a chuckle with Jim, his wit was prodigious and his store of jokes seemed endless. As Bob had been beset by worries, so Jim was relaxed and unruffled. The die was for the base of an American car, the Plymouth Plaza.

'Cut on the right side of the line, old son, otherwise it won't fit,' was his laconic remark as he handed me the job.

I went off to the band-saw, knowing that there wouldn't be any heavy breathing in my ear on this job.

And life grew even more rosy on that sunny afternoon. Again, at tea-break, Beverly was there, standing by the door laughing with her friends. I managed to catch her eye and smiled and was certain she smiled back. Then later on, a visit to the bog – I'd taken to going to the one nearer the Train Room – who should I meet but Beverly. Plucking up courage I smiled and said, as nonchalantly as I could, 'Hiya Beverly.' She looked a bit startled but smiled back in a funny sort of way and walked off up the passage.

And as we pushed our bikes through the crowds at knocking-off time – there she was again. With growing confidence I called, 'Goodnight Beverly.' Again that quizzical smile. A girl near her whispered something and they both giggled. It almost seemed as if fate was bringing us together.

I sprinted up the road in fine style; rode home in a dream; couldn't eat my tea and my restless dreams were filled with smiling, raven haired beauties.

The weekend held none of its usual appeal. Time dragged and I found myself constantly wondering what Beverly was doing. And during these musings, I was suddenly struck by an awful thought – supposing she already had a boyfriend?

Or even worse – she might even be engaged! Oh why hadn't I tried to see that telling finger? At least then I would have known one way or another. For once in my life I couldn't wait for Monday morning, and resolved to ask Beverly for a date at the first opportunity – ring or no ring!

I had never been in the factory so early. It was a strange experience leaning leisurely against the Toolroom door-post, watching the people drifting in, instead of belting up the passage, spurred on by the hooter's raucous summons. My sudden change of habit did not go unnoticed and I was subjected to all manner of sarcastic and ribald remarks until not feeling equal for the sustained barrage of wit at such an early hour, I abandoned my conspicuous post for the warm tranquillity of the Hardening Shop.

Abe's job was progressing well. My saw cut kissed the edge of the line in a perfect union, and as the morning progressed and the perfect union continued, I began to feel a certain smugness. What on earth had all the fuss been about? Cutting out precision dies presented no problem to the world's ace band-sawyer – the job was a doddle. And wait until my fore-man heard about another outstanding piece of work, I'd be his blue-eyed apprentice then alright!

Little did I realise that this would indeed be the case – but not in the way I anticipated.

Tea-break came and there she was, standing with her back to me, talking to her friends. As she stroked her hair I saw that all important finger – there was no ring.

'There's your bit of crumpet confided Chris, in my ear. 'When are you going to ask her out?'

'Oh I'll get round to it one of these days,' I responded airily, reluctant to admit that I was still infatuated.

'Well I'd hurry up if I were you,' he advised. 'Cos I know someone else who fancies her.'

I shot round. 'Who?'

He grinned, knowingly. 'Still keen eh? It's the apprentice in the Maintenance, Colin I think his name is. Know him?'

I nodded and relaxed a little. 'Him with the greasy hair and loads of pimples?'

'That's the one. We were at the Toolstores earlier and he spotted Beverly. She must have been going to the surgery. Got quite excited about her he did. Anyway I fixed him. Said she was engaged to a six foot docker who was dead jealous.'

We both laughed. 'Good lad,' I said warmly. 'I'll bet that put him off. Not that he'd have a chance anyway. I mean, what girl would go out with a walking pimple factory?'

We laughed again, then Chris nudged me. 'They're looking at us.'

I turned to see Beverly and her friends looking in. One of the girls said something and they all giggled before turning back to their conversation.

I felt slightly uneasy. 'What the bloody hell are they giggling at?'

He shrugged, 'I dunno.'

I had a horrible thought. 'You don't think they're laughing at us?'

'What!' he cried. 'A couple of handsome buggers like us – you must be joking!'

'In case you two handsome buggers hadn't noticed,' said a voice behind us, 'the queue's moved forward and I want my tea now, not this afternoon.'

We hurriedly closed the gap and the conversation turned to different topics.

I don't know exactly what caused it, other things on my

mind perhaps, but an hour or so later the band-saw blade cut through the metal quite suddenly and before I could release the pressure the whizzing teeth had nicked the line! I stared in disbelief, feeling sick with apprehension. What had I done!

Stopping the machine, I scrutinised the dreaded mark, but couldn't quite see if the line had indeed been cut through. I cursed myself for being so cocky and not concentrating and trying to collect my racing thoughts into some sort of rational order. So great was the shock that I'm sure that if no-one else had been around I would have wrung my hands in despair.

My first inclination, when I calmed down a bit, was to go and confess to Jim, but I dismissed this idea almost immediately. My machine was too close to the office and if Sinbad spotted Jim closely examining the die through a magnifying glass he would be bound to put two and two together. Equally I couldn't very well take the job to it's owner. As the blade had been joined through the middle of the metal, this solution would have meant going across to the other side of the Toolroom with yards of blade wobbling about all over the place, passing many pairs of curious eyes on the way. Perhaps the best way would be to break the blade and smuggle the die to Jim, but it was risky. What I desperately needed was a magnifying glass so I could do my own scrutinising without attracting unwelcome attention. I didn't possess my own magnifying glass as my turn in the Tool Club queue had not yet arrived, so could I borrow a glass from someone I could trust not to blab the news of my cock-up all over the Toolroom.

To give myself time to think, I restarted the machine and tried to continue working, but it was no use, my nerves were shot to pieces and no matter how I tried to ignore that fateful nick, my gaze was constantly drawn back, and every time the mistake looked more serious. At this rate I was bound to make another mistake, possibly even worse. Finally I pressed the red stop button to stop the machine so I could go off somewhere quiet and shoot myself.

As the saw slowly puffed to a stop Ken Edwards came strolling up the passageway.

He was one of the older apprentices, Tall and slim, with sandy hair and large horn-rimmed glasses, he was always immaculately dressed and looked more like a business executive than a budding toolmaker. His father was a senior manager in the factory and Ken drove him to work every morning. Fast driving, girls and backing horses were Ken's main interest but he was also a merciless practical joker.

In my panic I forgot about this, thinking only of the need to end my misery one way or another. A quick glance at the office showed Sinbad was out. This was my opportunity.

'Hey Ken! Could I borrow your eyeglass for a minute?'

He looked from me to the silent machine. 'Cocked it up have you?'

I felt my face go scarlet. 'No – at least I hope not. Got a bit close to the line that's all. Just thought I'd better check to be on the safe side.'

'Let's have a look.' He leant over the machine table, peering at the die. 'That's nasty.'

My heart sank.

'But it might be okay.'

My heart rose again.

He stood up. 'I'll get my eyeglass just to be sure.'

'I'll come over,' I offered.

He waved a dismissive hand. 'No, it's okay. I'll drop it off – I'm going to the stores anyway.

And don't worry,' he said, with a disarming grin. 'I won't go blabbing. Back in a minute.'

I started the saw again to look busy and avoid attracting attention. A couple of minutes later, out of the corner of my eye, I saw a flash of white as Sinbad came in the door, and simultaneously a watchmaker's eyeglass was neatly deposited on the band-saw table.

A quick look round, the foreman was talking at the front bench. Holding the small, black tube against my eye, I examined the damage. The magnified saw cut sprang into focus, the metal looking torn and jagged through the powerful lens. Then I found the mark and all those half-formed ideas of suicide vanished – most of that all-important line was still there. I hadn't cocked it up after all.

To celebrate I went off to the top bog to have a relaxing sit around on the wash basins to recover from my ordeal, and have a chat to any friends who might also be having a rest from their labours. As I neared the end of the corridor a small, familiar figure came walking towards me. It was Beverly! This was my chance. It was now or never!

Heart pounding like a trip hammer, I confronted her. 'Excuse me Beverly, but I wondered if you would like to come to the pictures with me one night?'

For an eternity she looked at me, then she laughed. 'Fuck off rat face! An' me name's not Beverly – it's Edna!' Then she was gone.

The world reeled! My romantic dreams crashed and fell in ruins as the words sank in. Her reply was so totally unexpected and cruel, that I could hardly believe what I had heard. That those luscious lips could utter such words, and to me her worshipping slave, was beyond all understanding. 'Fuck off rat face!' to me of all people! And her name wasn't even Beverly – it was common or garden bloody Edna! I tottered off to the bog needing that sit down more than ever.

But even the normally convivial atmosphere of the toilets seemed tainted on that dreadful morning. It was almost as if everyone knew what had happened, for I was the obvious centre of much grinning, elbow knocking and whispered asides. I didn't stay long, and as I wandered back to the Toolroom, I was treated to smirks and chuckles from everyone I passed. It was all very odd.

Lost in my misery I almost collided with Sinbad as I turned in the doorway. 'Sorry.' I mumbled, side stepping past him. He nodded acknowledgement and his lips tightened as though suppressing a smile. This was unnerving – even my foreman was at it now. What on earth was it about me that inspired such mirth in everyone I met?

I put my hand in my overall pocket for a wiper to clean the band-saw table. My fingers closed about the small, tube of Ken's eyeglass. With a sinking heart I realised what must had caused all those grins and smirks. I didn't want to believe it but when I ran my fingers round the black, flared eye-piece and a blue smear appeared on the skin, I knew I was right. A brief look in my small mirror from my tool box confirmed my worst fears. Completely encircling my right eye was a vivid blue ring. The old trick of smearing Engineer's Blue on the eyeglass and I'd fallen for it hook, line and sinker. It was no wonder that Beverly, no bloody Edna, had laughed, the rotten bitch. I could almost hear her giggling about it with that ferret-faced scrubber with the curlers as they merrily riveted the wheels on Dinky Toys. Well bugger them! There was nothing I could do about it now, and if that's the type she was, then good riddance.

For the rest of the morning I shut it all out of my mind by fiercely concentrating on Abe's die, determined not to make another mistake.

At lunch-time I returned Ken's eyeglass, cleaned and intact, although I almost succumbed to a desire to see how many small pieces I could cut it into.

'Thanks Ken,' I said airily, placing the glass on his bench.

'Everything all right?' he asked, grinning like a Cheshire cat.

Keeping a tight grip on my feelings I answered, mildly. 'That was a lousy trick to play when I was in such a state about that die.'

He ruffled my hair. 'Not at all. I knew the job was okay when I first looked at it. Just thought I'd have a bit of fun that's all. Did it get you?'

'Yes,' I replied shortly. There was no point in a denial, my startling blue eye had been seen by too many people.

He rubbed his hands together gleefully, but before he had chance to rub more salt into my wounded feelings, I cleared off to wash my hands.

And, of course, word had spread. My entrance to the crowded toilet was greeted by cheers and cries of – 'Who's the blue-eyed boy then!'

I was expected to laugh – so I did. It showed I could take a joke and didn't in the least mind about being made to look a complete twerp. 'Thou shalt grin and bear it.' was the young apprentices first commandment, so I grinned and bore it whilst I waited my turn at the wash basins, but inwardly I was seething and vowing to have revenge.

But not everyone was keen to rub it in. I still had friends who could be relied upon for a bit of morale boosting when the going got rough. Chris joined me at the basins in the now almost deserted toilets.

'I heard about the joke.'

'Oh aye,' I replied, and we both laughed.

'Who was it?'

'Kenny Edwards.'

He nodded. 'It would be.'

'Oh it's not that I mind the joke,' I said. 'What needles me is the rotten way he did it.'

'How's that?'

'You know that press tool die I'm cutting out for Jim Tullo?' He nodded. 'Well I cut into the line.'

He gave a whistle. 'Did you cock it up?'

'No! Thank God! But I was dead worried, I don't mind telling you. I couldn't see if the line was cut through and Kenny was passing so I asked him for a loan of his eyeglass.'

He frowned. 'Stupid.'

'Yes I know, but I was panicking like hell and never thought he'd pull a stunt like that when I was so upset.'

'Typical. You want to get him back somehow. Teach him a lesson.'

After my traumatic morning I didn't much feel like getting anyone back. 'I'll think about it.'

'Well sing out if you want any help,' he said, drying his hands. 'I've got a few scores to settle in that direction myself. Are you coming?'

'I'll just have a leak.'

'See you back there then. I've got a tin of soup on the furnace.'

As Chris went out, Johno came in. He didn't like me much and the feeling was mutual.

'Well, well, well. If it isn't our little blue-eyed boy,' he sneered. 'I believe you've been going round making a prick of yourself.'

This was the last straw! He was the one who'd told me the wrong name for the girl in the first place and made me look a complete fool. My resentment surfaced in an echo of Edna's response.

'Fuck off!'

Instantly my lapels were grabbed and I was slammed against the tiles with a force that knocked most of the breath out of my body. Johno towered over me, his face contorted with rage. 'Don't you ever tell me to fuck off, you little shrimp – or I'll put you in hospital!'

I struggled to get away, but it was futile. I was a little shrimp.

He slammed me against the tiles again. 'Got it!'

'Okay. Okay.' I gurgled.

The grip relaxed. 'Now get out!'

I went. Somehow it just wasn't my day. But as I walked back to the Toolroom Johno's words echoed through my mind. Maybe I was a little shrimp, but I was getting bigger all the time, and then we'd see Johno, then we'd see!

For weeks I was an avid woman hater. Where previously I'd made every effort to meet that bloody Edna, now I avoided her like the plague. I started bring a thermos flask of tea, as standing in the tea queue had become a nightmare of giggling stares from the passage outside. Perplexed by my sudden change of habit, my friends made strenuous efforts to discover the reason, but it was a long time before I admitted the painful truth. The only light in an otherwise gloomy world was that Jim's job had been finished without further mishap. But now my moment of glory was over – I was back on spray holders.

The Anna Anomaly

Cupid got me again, on the rebound I suppose, when my hatred of all things female had begun to wane.

I was at the Toolstores counter when Anna came up. She worked in the offices and came to the Stores a few times a week to collect paperwork. Tall and slim, with short, blonde hair, she was almost the exact opposite of my previous heart-throb. I'd seen her many times without any amorous spark being kindled in my breast, but today was different. Today, for some inexplicable reason, her nearness sent my pulse-rate climbing.

For the first time I noticed her long, slender hands as she leafed through the papers lying on the counter. For the first time I saw the shine on her hair; the small, shell-like ears with tiny blue earrings, in the shape of flowers and the graceful curve of her smooth neck, and, for the second time in my apprentice life, I was in love.

She stood up, taller than me in her stiletto heels, and gathered up the papers.

I smiled my best smile. 'Morning, Anna.'

She turned, looking faintly surprised, then with a brief: 'Oh. Good morning.' she was gone, walking rapidly away down the corridor.

I leant against the counter gazing dreamily after her until she turned the corner and the sharp tap of her heels faded in the Press Shop's rhythmic clamour.

'Fancy her do you?'

Mike's voice in my ear brought me abruptly down to earth.

I was giving nothing away.

'She's alright I suppose.'

'Snooty!' he informed me. 'Dead snooty! they're all the same these office birds. Think the sun shines out of their arses.'

I wasn't having that. 'That's because you're a yobbo and don't know how to treat a smart girl. If I was an office bird I wouldn't bother with a scruffy erk like you either. You haven't even got a tie on to hide your dirty neck.'

He grinned. 'Well you'll find out. Just you ask her for a date and see what happens. I'll bet you five bob she tells you to get stuffed.'

I wasn't having that either. 'She would to you,' I retorted, 'except she wouldn't use language like that. She's not one of your scrubbers. She's a nice girl.'

He leered. 'They're all nice in bed!'

Bill Cherry's voice brought the conversation to an abrupt halt. 'What's going on there? Yap! Yap! Yap! You're paid to work – not talk! Have you sorted that silver steel out yet Mike?'

Mike hurriedly handed me the drill I needed. 'Er, nearly Bill. Be about half an hour.'

'Well get on with it!' came the snapped command. 'And you clear off to your own department before I report you. Yap! Yap! Yap! It's a wonder you apprentices ever learn anything with all the talking you do!'

I went quietly without a word. When the volatile boss of the stores was in one of his moods it was the wisest thing to do.

Out of the frying pan ... A white coated figure was standing by my bench lathe. I hurried up, brandishing my drill like a flag of truce. I brandished in vain. The bullets were already on the way.

'Where have you been!' snapped the foreman.

'Er. To the stores for this drill.'

Fingers drummed impatiently on the bench. I gave you that requisition over fifteen minutes ago and saw you go out with it. I take it they haven't moved the Tool Stores?'

'No.' I answered, miserably.

'Then why have you been so long?'

I clutched a well-used lifebelt. 'I had to go to the bo..toilet.'

The glasses glinted accusingly at the lie. I squirmed during a long, inquisitive pause.

Then Sinbad said, 'Hmm. I'll take your word for it ... this time.' Emphasising 'this time' to show he knew I was lying. 'But in future we'll have less talking round the factory and more time spent in the Toolroom. I've had complaints about apprentices wasting time talking in other departments, and...' he paused again, 'if I have any more complaints ... '

He didn't finish, he didn't need to – the threat was unmistakable.

I worked like a demon, drilling and turning spray holders until the lunch-time hooter called a welcome break, and during the ritual examination of our sandwich contents, I discovered – much to my relief – that our foreman had paid more than one visit that morning.

'I've has complaints about apprentices talking,' mimicked Chris. 'And if I have any more complaints.' He took a vicious bite out his sandwich. It's like being back in bloody school! Please sir, he's been talking in class again.'

Andy hadn't escape the crack-down. 'I got it as well. Like the bloody Gestapo.'

Freddie brushed the crumbs of his knees. 'Well there's no need to spit half your butty over me.' Then he smirked. 'Anyway he didn't come to me, so that proves something.'

'It proves you're a bloody arse creeper,' retorted Chris, scathingly. 'I've heard you: Yes Mister Simpson. No Mister Simpson. Would you like me to polish your shoes Mister Simpson? Arse creeper!'

Freddie flushed. 'You lying hound! You've never heard me say that! You know very well I'm not an arse creeper!'

'Alright, alright,' laughed Chris. 'Just pulling your pisser. I wonder if our beloved foreman went to Bas, or Gordon or Gerry?'

'Shouldn't think so,' I said. 'They don't step out of line much.'

We thought about this. 'Bas might,' offered Andy, 'but I don't think Gordon or Gerry would, they're too quiet.'

There was a brief silence, then Andy said. 'I'd like to know who dropped us in it – the rotten bastard!'

We murmured agreement. I had a thought. 'I wonder if it was Bill Cherry?'

'Bill Cherry?' repeated Chris. 'He wouldn't pull a stunt like that. What makes you think it might be him?'

'Oh,' I said. 'I was at the Stores talking to Mike and Bill was in a right old mood and lost his rag. Started shouting about reporting me; but you're right, he'd never do it.'

And neither would he. Although, at times, Bill could erupt like a volcano and bluster and threaten, at heart he was a kindly soul and wouldn't knowingly drop anyone in the cart. No! It definitely wasn't Bill.

So we sat and munched and swigged our tea and thought of likely suspects, which was a bit of a waste of time really. Even if we discovered who had dropped us in it, apart from giving the culprit, (or culprits), dirty looks and telling an uncaring world of who had dropped us in it, there was little we could do. My thoughts strayed in other directions

– female directions.

'Tell you who I saw at the Stores. I said.

Andy looked up from cleaning his nails with the corner of his steel rule. 'Who?'

'Anna. You know, that little blonde cracker from the office.'

'Anna?' He echoed. 'A little cracker? You must be joking! She's dead snooty for one thing.'

'And she's got no tits,' said Freddie, with satisfaction.

'And she's bandy,' added Chris, not to be outdone.

All of which may well have been true. But I was in love, and love is blind, so I argued fiercely on Anna's behalf, and wished I'd kept my mouth shut.

'Tell you one thing though,' remarked Chris, as the argument petered out and we got ready for a walk up Binns Road. 'I happen to know that Stan asked Anna for a date a couple of months ago.'

This was news – and unwelcome.

'What did she say?' asked Andy.

Chris grinned. 'Apparently, she looked down her nose, said, 'No thank you, I'm fussy who I go out with, and walked off'.

We guffawed loudly. It was well known that our fellow apprentice considered himself something of a lady killer.

Freddie slid the door open. 'I'll bet he was choked,' he chortled, as we trooped out into the corridor.

The door slid shut with a soft thud. I asked Chris the obvious question. 'How did you find out about all this?'

'Mike,' he answered. 'There's not much goes on around the Stores that he doesn't know about.'

I made a mental note not to trust Mike in future.

A week later I was leaning against the cupboard by the Dekel Miller, slitting the fruits of my labours on the bench lathe. The autumn sun was streaming through the glass in the shadow roofing was warm on my back. Someone's toneless whistling of *How Much Is That Doggie In The Window* rose above the hum of machines, until the owner of a more tuneful ear called for him to: 'Put a sock in it.'

I was happy, and – despite the spray holders – reasonably content. I say reasonably because no adolescent can be totally content – nature decrees otherwise, and the glittering gifts of the adult world constantly beckon. But, on the whole, I was as content as I was likely to be at sixteen and a bit. I knew I was lucky to be part of Meccano, and serving my time in this unique factory whose Toolroom had a reputation second to none. And I was also fortunate to have such friends and work-mates – give or take a few. So I leaned against the cupboard and had a go at whistling myself.

I was still whistling when Chris came in.

'Anna's at the Stores if you're interested,' he said as he passed.

The whistle was instantly swamped by a sea of indecision. Should I or shouldn't I?

The wounds inflicted by Edna were still painful, but Anna was different. She wasn't a scrubber, and even if she did say no it would be in a nice way, so what had I got to lose? Quickly straightening my tie, I ran a comb through my hair and, with a pounding heart, hurried through the door.

And there she was, leafing through the papers on the counter – and she looked gorgeous. I sidled up, eyes fixed on the short, blonde hair, and reached her side as she stood up.

'Morning, Anna,' I croaked.

She looked at me, unsmiling. 'Oh hello,' and picking up the papers she turned to go.

'Anna!' I said desperately.

She turned, enquiringly. 'Yes?'

The words tumbled out. 'Would you like to go to the pictures with me one night?'

From her stiletto-heeled height she stared down at me. 'No I wouldn't!' she said scornfully. 'I don't go in for baby snatching!'

Once again I could hardly believe my ears; and once again my romantic dreams withered and died on a sharp and heartless tongue. But this time at least I had a small revenge. My friends had been right about Anna. She was dead snooty, she was certainly flat-chested and, as she teetered down the passage on those ridiculous high heels, I could see that she was very definitely bandy.

Gathering the few remaining shreds of my dignity, I trudged back to the Toolroom.

I had no idea if Mike had overheard my humiliation and I didn't really care. The opposite sex appeared to regard me as a rat-faced baby, and if Mike wished to join their ranks by spreading the story abroad, then so be it! We are what we are and I could no more help my looks and being small, than Anna could help being bandy and flat-chested, and Edna being a mindless scrubber.

But I still had feelings and was not prepared to risk having them trampled on again by another heartless female's hob-nailed boots. From now on I was finished with the opposite sex, and if I stayed a virgin for the rest of my life, then so be that as well. But life is strange and I could only see my side of the situation; the unanswered question, which I hadn't even thought of was: had the opposite sex finished with me?'

There was no secrecy this time. At the first available opportunity I related the story to the lads, and to my surprise there was none of the jeering remarks I'd half expected. Instead there was outraged indignity that one of their number could be treated so shabbily and the phrase, 'bloody bitch' was frequently heard. Then the ranks closed against the perpetrator and suggestions made for how she could be made to pay for her crime.

To my credit I did my best to persuade my friends to forget the whole thing, preferring to let the incident drift into the past, where it rightly belonged, but the lust for blood was up and the pack would not relent until they had seen its colour. Although she had rightly been christened: The bloody bitch, I began to feel slightly sorry for Anna.

Lunch-time the following day was bright and sunny. We strolled leisurely down Binns Road towards the factory, enjoying the sunshine, eyeing the talent and discussing a subject dear to all our hearts – motorbikes. Although I still loved my Claude Butler, and had great times going out with the factory cycling club, called the Cygnet Wheelers, like my friends, I now lived for the day when, helmeted and goggled, I would scorch down that long hill in a blast of glorious sound that would turn every head for miles around. But somehow today the magic of Triumph and Norton, Matchless, AJS and BSA was missing. Even my friends seemed restless. Then we heard the loud tapping of heels above the general chatter, and Anna came hurrying past. 'Well, well,' said Chris. 'Look who's here!'

The three of them took off like hounds on the scent, leaving me behind and not involved in whatever was going to happen next.

Andy had first bite. 'It is Anna I tell you,' he said loudly. 'I'd recognise those bandy legs anywhere.'

The victim threw a hurried glance over her shoulder and quickened her pace, but there was no escape.

'That's a rotten thing to say,' mocked Chris, equally loudly.

'She can't help being bandy, anymore than she can help being flat-chested.'

'And I've heard she's dead snooty,' called Freddie, as the victim quickened her pace even more.

Practically running now she disappeared through the crowd and I caught up with my friends.

'That fixed her, the rotten bitch!' said Andy. 'She might think twice now before she's nasty to people.'

'Boy!' cried Freddie. 'Was she embarrassed. The back of her scrawny neck was bright red.'

'She was nearly running by the time she reached the gate,' enthused Chris. 'Her legs were going up and down like the con-rods on a five hundred twin at full chat.'

We all guffawed loudly. Justice had been done. Honour satisfied, and the opposite sex had been put firmly in its place – and who needed girls anyway! Like conquering heroes we swaggered through the gate to clock on.

The result of that little skirmish was that shortly afterwards a different girl started coming to the Toolstores to collect the paperwork. We never discovered the reason for this sudden change.

I was back on the bandsaw, cutting up various pieces of steel into various shapes for various toolmakers. The job I was currently working on was thick metal so the saw blade's progression through the steel was almost imperceptible. For just such a situation there was a tension device which kept the job constantly pressing against the teeth of the blade, leaving the operator with little to do except to guide the metal from time to time to keep the cut on course.

As I peered at the line a small filing suddenly flicked into my eye, a not uncommon occurrence if the operator was not wearing goggles – something very few people did as they were uncomfortable and had an annoying habit of misting up. Going to my nearby toolbox, I got my little mirror and returned to the machine whilst I removed the irritating grain with the corner of my handkerchief.

I was rather proud of that mirror; it was quite a unique little thing.

Some time ago the hinges on my mum's powder compact had broken and when even my dad's considerable engineering ingenuity had failed to repair the fault, I had saved it from going in the bin. The mirror was backed with highly polished brass with the name STRATTON inlaid in black, and was very superior to the broken mirror scraps owned by most of my fellow apprentices.

A shaft of sunlight, suddenly illuminated the table, flashing off the mirror and giving me an idea of how to relieve my boredom – for a while at least. By tilting the mirror in the sunbeam a small, brilliant spot of light could be made to dance on the wall, a machine or best of all around some unsuspecting toolmakers head. It was great sport, and while the bandsaw whirred and puffed, busily doing my job for me, I caused minor chaos along the rows of benches.

My little spotlight finally alighted on George Burton, a rather dour individual whose sombre expression rarely changed. The Toolroom's comedians had given up on George. If he was told an hilarious story, which had most of us falling about, laughing hysterically, long after the punch-line had been delivered George would continue to stare dourly at the joke teller as if he was still waiting for the funny part to arrive.

He was an industrious worker and when my little spot danced up to him he was busily filing. A quick flash across the eyes had him looking up questioningly, but hidden behind my bandsaw bunker, I'd already doused the light.

After a short time, looking about, he resumed his filing. I gave him a minute or so then struck again – with the same result, only this time it took him longer to recover. This was great stuff to tell the lads at break time, how I'd had old Georgie crawling up the wall. For the next few minutes I had a field day, periodically sending my brilliant shaft lancing across the Toolroom and sniggering delightedly at George's increasingly exasperated reactions, as he glowered round trying to find the source of the irritation. Then I had to abandon the project as the line on my job reached a curve which demanded my full attention.

Shortly afterwards I was aware of a movement behind me and felt a hand go into my overall pocket. I looked round into George's sombre face as he withdrew his hand, holing my treasured mirror. Without a word, he placed it on the band-saw table and hit it once with the hammer he was carrying in his other hand. Still without a word he walked away towards his bench.

He was a good shot. Beneath its mangled, brass casing that mirror was in at least a thousand pieces.

The retribution metered out to Anna by my friends, had made me realise that revenge, even by proxy, is sweet and a good confidence builder. So with my prospective sweetheart safely disposed of, I determined to show the lads that I could now stand alone, by settling my outstanding score with Ken Edwards for the blue eyeglass episode.

Enough time had elapsed since the incident to enable me to retaliate without being immediately pinpointed as the culprit, thus avoiding a tit-for-tat situation which I would be certain to lose. The fact that, (hopefully), Kenny would not know who had fixed him was not important. What ultimately mattered was ensuring that his discomfiture was viewed by many but the identity of the perpetrator of the crime was known only to a select few. And working on the bandsaw was good. By peering under the casing of the top wheel I would have a good view of my victim without being seen myself, so I could watch the outcome of my revenge in comparative safety.

I made the announcement at morning tea-break. 'I'm gonna get Kenny Edwards.'

Immediately there was a stir of interest.

'When?' demanded Chris.

'At lunch-time, so long as there's no one around.'

'What are you going to do?' asked Freddie, stirring his tea vigorously with his steel rule. 'Nail his tools to the bench?'

'That'll make your rule go black,' Chris informed him, 'and you won't be able to see the marks.'

'It wouldn't make any difference to him,' scoffed Andy. 'He only works to the nearest half inch anyway.' He dodged as Freddie flicked the tea off the rule in his direction.

'I thought I'd blue him up,' I said.

They all nodded agreement with this suggestion.

'Blue his bollocks,' said Freddie, enthusiastically. 'Get his sleeves gripped between two vice and you've got him – he can't do a thing!'

'Except kick you in the bollocks,' observed Chris. 'He's still got feet you know.'

Grinning, Freddie gave him a deliberate V sign.

Andy decided it was time to boost my confidence. 'I wouldn't like to be in your shoes if he finds out who did it. He can be a nasty bastard can Kenny – him and Tony Smith could make your life a bloody misery.'

'That wouldn't bother me,' I said with more bravado than I was feeling. 'Even if he did find out it was me, there's not much he could do about it except blue me again.'

Freddie was also on the confidence building bus. 'Oh isn't there? He could get some of his mates and stick your head down the bog for a start. Johno would love that.'

I hadn't thought of that particularly nasty form of punishment, and although I'd heard it used as a threat against an apprentice who'd overstepped the mark, I'd never known the threat to be carried out – but there was always a first time. Once again I found myself wishing I'd kept my mouth shut. Anna's retribution had been a mere minnow, blueing Kenny was a dive into shark tank. But there was no going back now without appearing cowardly in the eyes of my friends and that was unthinkable. So I had no choice but to carry out my plan and hope and pray that I didn't get caught in the act.

By lunch-time I was very nearly a nervous wreck. The remainder of my morning had been spent worrying about the event and hoping against hope that something unforeseen would happen to let me off the hook. I hoped in vain. Even the weather was against me for the sun streamed in through the roof windows, inviting everyone to take a lunch-time walk or fiddle with their cars or motorbikes.

The hooter blared like a siren of doom. The factory noises dwindled and died and my hopes dwindled and died with them. I didn't bother to wash my hands, I'd have to wash them after the blueing job and I didn't want to bump into my victim in the bog – that would have finished me altogether. So I sat miserable eating – or trying to eat – sawdust sandwiches until my excited friends joined me.

'All set?' asked Chris, as he sat down.

I nodded dumbly, vainly trying to swallow whatever it was I'd been chewing for the last five minutes.

Freddie gleefully rubbed his hands together gleefully. 'I can't wait,' he chortled. 'It's about time we got some of those bastards back.'

'What's this 'we' business?' I asked, coldly. 'I'm the one who's doing the dirty work, you're having nothing to do with it – unless you'd like to swap places.'

'No! No!' he said hastily. 'I just meant … ' He tailed off, opening his sandwich box. 'Bloody hell! I don't know what I mean.'

'Have you got the Blue?' asked Andy.

I was off the hook. In my worrying I'd forgotten all about it.

'Bloody hell!' I replied, happily. 'I'd forgotten all about it.'

From his overall pocket he produced a small tin of Engineer's Blue. 'I borrowed this in case you forgot.'

'Thanks a lot,' I said, sarcastically, taking the tin. 'I'm glad you remembered.'

He grinned. 'We aim to please.'

Giving up on my sandwiches – the dog could have them when I got home – I watched gloomily as my last hopes of reprieve finished their lunches and strolled out through the door. Until finally, with the exception of a few senior members, engrossed in their *Daily Sketches, Mirrors* or *Daily Heralds* the Toolroom was empty.

'Okay Roy,' growled Chris in a Humphrey Bogart voice, 'the coast's clear – go and get him!'

'Alright! Alright!' I said, testily. 'I'm going. Will you guys keep lookout in case anyone comes?'

They nodded assent.

'If we see anyone we'll whistle,' said Humphrey Bogart, in a conspirital whisper. 'One for Sinbad; two for Edwards; three for … '

'Very funny,' I interrupted. 'Just whistle once.'

Andy heaved a sigh. 'If you wait much longer they'll all be

back and we'll be whistling our bloody heads off.'

I clutched at the straw. 'Perhaps you're right. It might be better if—'

'Go on!' interrupted Chris. 'Bugger off and do it!'

And, wishing I was anywhere but there, I went.

By the time I reached Kenny's bench I was in a cold sweat, imagining hidden, hostile eyes watching my every move. I had a quick look round. A little further along George was reading a news paper spread out on his bench. He paid me no attention.

I hesitated for a moment, then turned my attention to the tools lying on the bench. Even if he saw me George wouldn't spill the beans, he never got involved in any of the Toolroom's intrigues.

There were a number of tools scattered about, so I did them all. I blued the vice handle (always a favourite), the underside of the hammer shaft and file handles and, for good measure, the little black knobs on the tool cabinet drawers. Then, like a thief in the night, I scuttled back to my friends.

'How did it go?', asked Freddie, excitedly, as we walked smartly down the corridor to the bog.

Now that the deed was done I felt quite heroic. 'No problem,' I boasted. 'I did the lot! His vice handle; his hammer and his file handles, and,' I was rather proud of this one, the little knobs on his toolbox.'

Chris whistled. 'You cunning devil. I'd never have thought of that.'

Andy congratulated me. 'Well done, that'll teach him.'

Freddie rubbed his hands together, gleefully. 'I can't wait. I hope the bastard gets covered in it.'

I washed my hands carefully, ensuring not a trace of blue remained as incriminating evidence, then we went to the motorbike park to mingle with the lucky owners, admire the bikes and establish an alibi in case we were suspected of being involved in the blueing job.

All too soon we clocked on and drifted back to our work. The euphoria of actually accomplished my task had long since evaporated, now I was aghast at what I'd done and worried sick about the outcome. That toilet bowl loomed cold and menacing, and all because I wanted to act the big shot – I must have been mad!

Chris and Andy had good views of the crime scene, Chris from the big milling machine and Andy from his centre lathe. Freddie was on the bench now so it was up to him to pick a good spot.

It was fortunate I was only cutting a rough job. By the time I started the bandsaw my apprehension had reached such proportions that I felt sick and my hands were visibly trembling. For the hundredth time I berated myself for being a bloody fool and wished fervently that I could wave a magic wand and remove all that incriminating blue.

But I had no magic wand, so I could only wait until retribution came and tapped me on the shoulder, as I was certain it would. And, as if I hadn't suffered enough, fate decided to prolong the agony. Instead of starting work, Kenny went into the office to discuss something with Sinbad. I tried to concentrate but the condemned are incapable of concentration.

A movement at Kenny's bench caught my eye. It was Johno. I watched from behind my bandsaw shield as he fiddled with something. I couldn't see what he was doing for a shelf, about a foot high, fixed along the top of the benches, obscured my view. He walked away holding a file he had borrowed, which he tossed in the air intending to catch it as it spun round – but he didn't. Instead he let it fall as he gazed at his blue hand. A malicious smile crept across his face and picking up the file he walked slowly back to his bench, cleaning the handle with his wiper.

The bandsaw hummed and puffed and still I watched, holding the metal loosely against the blade so it looked as if I was working. What would Johno do? Would he tell Kenny? I hoped so, for then the whole affair would fizzle out with little harm done. Out of the corner of my eye I saw Kenny come out of the office. 'Go on Johno,' I willed. 'Tell.' And tell he did but not in the way I'd hoped.

To my horror he went on a high speed trip along the benches whispering a few quick words in each waiting ear, and by the time my victim arrived back at his bench, practically the entire Toolroom knew what was lying in wait for him. Never had I seen so many eyes watching without appearing to be watching. It was like some awful nightmare play – and I was the one who had set the stage.

Transfixed I watched and waited – so did everyone else. But fate was having a field day with me. As I held my breath for the appearance of the first blue splodge, Kenny walked over to one of the pillar drills, which ran in a line between the lines of benches, and began drilling a block of metal. The anticlimax turned my knees to water and I clung to the vibrating bandsaw table like a drowning man clings to a life-raft.

But the stay of execution was short-lived. A few minutes later Kenny came back to his bench with the block of steel, clamped it in the vice and picked up a file. I swallowed hard. the deed was done – there was no going back now.

He filed busily for a while, then putting the tool down he wiped the sweat from his forehead, his forehead came out in a rash of blue streaks. He pushed his glasses further on to his nose, his nose turned blue. The rows of benches were lit by broad grins and laughter floated above the drone of machines. Another spate of filing climaxed with some tie straightening, leaving me fervently hoping his mother would be able to wash his blue collar white again.

An itching ear was soon cured by turning it blue. Then he decided to light a blue cigarette and it was all over. Well not quite, as he held the cigarette out in front of him, realisation dawning on his face, the Toolroom erupted in a cacophony of cheering and hammers being banged on benches. I saw Sinbad standing up in the office to see what all the noise was about and applied myself so vigorously to my work that I nearly stopped the bandsaw blade.

And I couldn't help chuckling myself – and feeling a little proud. If a price had to be paid for my deed, then it was worth it. For the first time I had hit back on my own and succeeded

gloriously, and whatever else might happen one thing was certain – the rat-faced baby was gone forever.

As the afternoon wore on my feelings alternated between heroic heights and dark despair.

I worked as mechanically as the saw, hardly even seeing the steel as vivid pictures of Kenny's blue nose and ruined shirt switch-backed through my mind.

Sinbad walked past, pausing briefly to look over my shoulder at the job, before continuing along the passage and out into the main corridor. I watched him go, wondering if he suspected something, or if he was keeping an eye on me for some other reason – either way I'd soon find out.

'Hello little boy blue,' murmured a voice in my ear.

My heart almost stopped and I jumped so violently with shock and fright that I rammed the metal into the blade, making it squeal in protest. The moment I'd dreaded had arrived early.

I whipped round, almost inarticulate in my panic. 'Wah! Why! What the bloody hell did you do that for! I nearly cut my bloody finger off!' I shouted.

Kenny smiled – a faintly blue, menacing smile – underlined by his deep blue collar. 'I didn't do anything,' he said softly. 'I simply said, "Hello little boy blue." Why did you jump? Guilty conscience?'

I didn't like this soft stuff one little bit, it was unnerving. He should have been frothing at the mouth after what I'd done to him. Was it possible he knew I was the culprit and he was playing some sinister game of cat and mouse? I tried to brazen it out.

'You're enough to make anybody jump, sneaking up like that,' I blustered. 'And what's all this little boy blue business? It's a bloody stupid thing to say if you ask me.'

He stared me straight in the eye. 'Was it you?'

My heart was racing like a motorbike engine but I wasn't giving up yet. 'Was what me?'

'You know.'

'No I don't.'

'Then I'll spell it out for you. Was it you who blued every bloody tool on my bench and got me in this mess?'

Suddenly I didn't care any more. 'Yes it bloody well was!' I shouted. 'You had it coming and it serves you bloody well right!'

And to my amazement, and heartfelt relief – he grinned. 'I thought it was.'

'But aren't you mad?' I asked incredulously.

He laughed and clapped me on the shoulder. 'Not now. I've just found out I've won two hundred quid on the gee-gees.'

'Two hundred quid!' I gasped. It was a fortune.

'A double Yankee.' he explained, airily.

'And no hard feelings?'

He laughed again. 'To be honest I don't blame you after that eyeglass I pulled on you. But don't push your luck and try it again.'

I caught a flash of white near the door. 'Look out! here's Sinbad!'

Ken melted away between the machines. I carried on happily sawing. It was all over. Fate had decided to relent and let me off the hook. Life was looking good again.

For Chris, however, it was a different matter.

During lunch-time it was the practice of certain individuals, who brought their lunch wrapped in grease-proof paper, to roll the discarded paper tightly into a ball, then see if the resultant missile could be thrown with sufficient force and accuracy to decapitate an unsuspecting fellow worker. And it was Johno's practice, on spotting one of these discarded balls, to let out a mighty roar of 'Goal!' and boot the ball indiscriminately at friend and foe alike. He was no mean footballer was Johno; his aim was good, his kick powerful and being smacked violently on the ear by one of those penalty shots was something to be strenuously avoided. Many of us had felt the force behind Johno's right leg and loud and vociferous had been our protestations – but to no avail. The roar continued unchecked, bringing instant panic to all within range and it became second nature to duck whenever that dreaded cry rang out.

And it chanced one lunch-time, a few days after the blueing job, to have started raining heavily, bringing all the fresh air strollers and vehicle fiddlers hurrying back to the shelter of the factory. About eight of us apprentices had clocked on early and were standing in the Toolroom, gossiping, cracking jokes and watching the girls go by.

'The Goons are on tonight,' observed Gordon loudly, to no one in particular. the remark immediately bringing a chorus of: 'You dirty rotten swine!' interspersed with: 'Min, Min.' 'Yes Henry?' for most of us were fans of Eccles, Bluebottle and company.

'Look out! Here comes trouble!' warned a very passable impression of Grytpype Thyne - and he was right.

Flanked by two of his side-kicks, Bill Smith, amiable and a good saxophone player, and Jimmy Whitehouse, fiery and muscular, Johno sauntered in through the doorway. A rather wet Johno who'd evidentially been caught in the rain, and someone just couldn't resist it.

'He's fallen in the water,' came a Goonish wail from somewhere within our ranks.

Johno glared. 'Don't get smart with me!' And deliberately treading on a few of the nearest feet, he passed on.

We muttered and grumble and gave V signs to the retreating backs, but no-one was brave enough to risk being singled out by answering back out loud.

Gazing after them I noticed a large ball of paper lying invitingly on the floor. Johno saw it too and pivoting round he let fly a devastating drive in our direction. But it never happened. Instead, as the speeding foot connected with the intended projectile, there came a dull thud, the ball rolled sluggishly for a short distance and abruptly stopped. The war-cry, begun so triumphantly as 'Goal!' ended in a drawn-out 'A-a-a-ah!' of agony as, holding his injured foot, the would-be goal scorer pirouetted round and round like some demented ballet dancer.

There was a stunned silence, broken only by the wails of pain, as we slowly realised that something very nasty had happened to that foot. And then the laughter came, rising in volume and swamping the moans from that hopping pain-racked figure.

'You'd better go to the surgery,' said Bill, a worried expression on his face. 'You might have broken something.'

We hoped he had.

Johno tested his foot gingerly on the floor. 'Ouch!' he groaned, leaning on his friend's shoulder. He glared down at the source of his suffering. 'What the bloody hell is that? It was like kicking a lump of bloody lead.'

Bending down, Jimmy tugged at the paper. It peeled away like a skin, revealing a large, round lump of lead Mazak, the remains of one of the heavy weights used for tool testing. Someone obviously had a score to settle with the Toolroom's goal kicker.

Sniggering, we nudged each other gleefully with our elbows.

Johno looked down at the weight. '*BASTARDS!* If I find out who did that I'll— ' He stopped as if struck by a sudden thought and glowered at us suspiciously.

The sniggering died away as we received the full force of that searching glare. Feet shuffled nervously as, one by one, our faces were scrutinised for signs of guilt. As far as the victim was concerned we had all gathered together to witness the trap he had walked into so beautifully, therefore one of us must be the bastard who had set the trap.

Judge and jury, he reached a verdict and pronounced sentence.

'It's head down the bog for you Chris Thomas. I'll teach you not to mess with me!'

Sighs of relief whistled from everyone except Chris, and there was a general movement away from him as if he'd suddenly become contaminated – which he had in a way. He'd been singled out; set apart from the crowd and marked down for a nasty fate and no-one was prepared to risk sharing that fate by staying too close.

Chris recovered his power of speech. 'It wasn't me Ronnie!' he protested, stridently. 'Honestly. I knew nothing about the bloody thing until you kicked it – and that's God's truth.'

'Shurrup you little squirt. Of course it was you, standing there grinning your bloody stupid head off!'

Chris was fighting for his life. 'But I'm always grinning. I can't help it.'

Which was very true. Chris had the sort of round, cherubic face that looked merry even when he was miserable – and he was pretty miserable right now.

'It was you alright,' the executioner ground out, 'and you've had it!'

'But why should I be blamed for something I didn't do!' shouted Chris. 'It's bloody unfair!'

'Shurrup!' snapped Johno, and turned to hobble away.

And then I surprised myself. 'It wasn't him Ronnie! Pick on someone your own size.'

'Yeh!' cried Andy. 'That's right!'

'Yeh!' cried other voices as the mood caught. Tense, excited bodies jostled against each other as the apprentices surged forward; Chris wasn't alone now.

Bill's worried expression deepened; Jimmy flexed his muscles; Johno sneered.

'Fancy your chances do you?'

'Yeh!' we roared.

'Come on then! he invited. 'Who's gonna be first?' He spoke boldly but his face was tense with apprehension. This throng of youths, so easily intimidated moments before, had suddenly become a violent mob thirsting for hit blood.

In an attempt to avert disaster, Bill took a hurried pace forward, arm half outstretched as if to hold us back. 'Don't be daft fellas. We'll all end up getting the sack. Forget it.'

'Tell him to forget it then,' said Chris, insolently, secure in the support of his apprentice allies. 'I said I didn't do it – and that's the truth.'

Bill turned questioningly towards his friend. Johno passed a hand, almost wearily across his eyes, 'Okay,' he said heavily. 'Forget it – I'm sick of the whole business.' And, supported by his friends and wincing with every step, he reached the door and they disappeared down the corridor towards the surgery.

We watched in silence until they were out of sight, then the air was filled with whoops of jubilation; backs were slapped and shoulders punched as the tension drained away.

'Thanks fellas,' said Chris, but his words were lost in the long wail of the hooter. It was time to start work again.

Despite much talk, speculation and diligent detective work, no-one ever discovered who really planted that so-inviting, trouble causing ball of Mazak. It was a long time before: 'Goal!' rang out across the Toolroom again.

As the weeks went by and my dignity slowly recovered from the wounds inflicted by the cruel tongues of Anna and Edna (who appeared to have left as I hadn't seen her for some time), my determination to stay forever celibate began to weaken. Regardless of the reasons, attempting to remain indifferent to the charms of the opposite sex when you're young and randy, and for five days out of seven virtually surrounded by thousands of females is an almost impossible task. And my friends weren't helping matters either.

Chris had finally persuaded Big Tits from the Press Shop that she couldn't live without him; Andy was laying siege to a cracking red-head from the Train Room and Freddie was on chatting terms with a blonde armature winder who was built like an all-in wrestler.

But although I was rapidly coming to the conclusion that a monastic life was not for me, I was reluctant to stick my neck out again and risk it coming within range of yet another female wielding a verbal meat cleaver.

It was tempting, particularly as there seemed to have been a sudden influx of attractive young girls into Meccano's work force, but the risk was too great. Far better to stay frustrated an safe than to venture out into the hazards of that female jungle again. I had decided to finish with girls and for the foreseeable future, that's how it would stay. but, as I have stated earlier, that was my view of the situation. At least one member of the opposite sex had other ideas.

And Then There Was Rose

Besides Big Tits, or Mary as she had been christened, the Press Shop sported another girl of slightly erotic name – one Knicker Riley. In most respects Knicker differed little from the multitude of other teenage girls who worked in the factory. She was about five feet tall with red hair, good legs and a figure, hidden for most of the time by a green overall. What set her apart from the crowd was her make-up. Where many of the other girls unconcernedly sported curlers, head scarves, blotchy complexions and dark ringed eyes from last night's amorous adventures or booze ups – or both, Knicker was always made up, lip-sticked and mascara'd fit to kill, and she looked striking. How or why she came by her unusual title no-one – including Knicker herself – seemed to know, but far from being upset she seemed rather proud of her nickname.

Many theories had been advanced, over Toolroom mugs of tea, as to how she got her name, by far the most popular being that she didn't wear any, and Knicker was actually a shortened version of Knickerless, but as she had good humouredly refused all invitations to prove the theory one way or another, no-one knew for sure. Little did we suspect, as we mused and pondered over our mugs of tea, that I could be the one who could find out.

It was lunch-time, the sun was shining and I was trying to repair the broken rear carrier on my bike with some perforated strips from Meccano sets. Nearby an admiring crowd was gathered round Johno's new Royal Enfield Bullet motorbike, taking it in turns to fiddle wistfully with the controls whilst the proud owner looked on, loudly asserting that it would 'Do the ton – no problem.' Since the Mazak ball incident Johno had mellowed slightly.

'Shrimp' had all but disappeared from his vocabulary and a few minutes earlier I had been given the supreme thrill of being allowed to sit on his beautiful, gleaming machine whilst I did my own bit of wistful fiddling.

Chris emerged from the crowd and strolled over. 'How's it going?'

'I think it will hold,' I said, tightening a nut.

'You should have taken it off and asked Frank to weld it,' he observed. 'He'd have fixed it alright.'

I agreed. 'Yes I know, but some of the nuts are rusted and I can't get the bloody thing off.'

He watched idly as I bent the strip to shape. In the adjacent throng someone was baiting the Bullet's owner.

'Not much of a paint job,' sneered a voice. 'I've seen better finishes on Dinky Toys.'

Johno wasn't biting. 'I'm not surprised,' he sneered back, 'everyone knows you're half bloody blind!'

Chris laughed. 'They're taking the piss out of Johno.'

'Trying to,' I corrected. 'That's a belting motorbike. He let me sit on it earlier – it felt fantastic.'

He gave a heavy sigh. 'I know the feeling Just imagine the birds you could get with a bike like that.'

I tightened another nut. 'Talking of birds, how are you getting on with Big T ... er Mary?' I hastily corrected myself recalling, from past experiences, how the lustful pursuer had a nasty habit of suddenly turning into a doting, easily outraged boy friend. This wasn't the case with Chris.

'I'm not,' he said gloomily. 'The biggest tits in Liverpool and she wont let me near them.'

'Not even on the outside?' I asked incredulously.

'Not even on the outside,' he affirmed, even more gloomily. 'When I think of the money I've spent carting her off to the pictures – and all for nothing. The other night I got bloody soaked waiting for the bus home, it makes you sick.'

'How does she manage to stop you?' I asked, fishing for the interesting details.

He snorted. 'Well might you ask! She's like a bloody eel, wriggling about all over the place and giggling, 'Stop it Chris, I'm not like that,' all the bloody time. She's always giggling. I'll give it one last go and if I don't get them out then she's had it!'

There was a sudden roar as the Bullet's engine was kicked into life. We looked over to see Andy sitting triumphantly on the pillion as Johno took him for a ride up the road.

'Lucky bugger,' remarked Chris, as the roar faded in the distance. 'Has he told you how he's getting on with that bird from the Train Room?'

'No,' I said. 'He doesn't say anything about her – to me anyway.'

He pulled a face. 'Nor to me. He must be in love, the silly bugger. He'll be sorry when she starts stopping at every jeweller's window to look at engagement rings.'

I stood up and dropped the tools into my overall pocket. 'Well that's his problem. I'm staying single and wouldn't be interested even if they started waving their knickers at me.'

'That's it!' he exclaimed, grinning from ear to ear. 'I knew there was something I had to tell you.'

I didn't like that big grin. 'What's that?' I asked, suspiciously.

His grin widened even further as he dropped his bombshell. 'Knicker Riley wants you to take her out!'

For a few long, shocked seconds I stared at the grinning face as my mind grappled with the startling message. Then the crescendo of the Bullet's exhaust as it flashed past the gate, galvanised me into verbal action. 'Knicker Riley?' I croaked. 'Wants *me* to take her out?'

'Yep!' smirked the messenger.

'But ... What! ... How do you know?' I stuttered.

'Mary told me. Knicker asked her to ask me to ask you if you would take her out.'

I repeated the words slowly. 'Knicker asked Mary to ask you to ask me ... Is this on the level?'

'Gospel.'

I still didn't trust him. 'How gospel?'

'Five quid,' he replied promptly.

With two weeks wages up front I had to believe him, and now I'd recovered from the initial shock, I began to feel a bit peeved about this third-hand invitation. For a start it wasn't the done thing. Girls didn't simply up and ask a fellow to take them out just like that. Asking for a date was our prerogative. If a girl fancied a boy she was supposed to giggle and flutter her eyelashes and keep bumping into him accidentally on purpose, until he got the message. Then, if he fancied her, he'd ask for a date. If he didn't bite the apple, she would eventually get the message and look for someone else to giggle and flutter at. Besides, half the factory appeared to be in on the act, and I wasn't prepared to conduct my love affairs under the prying eyes of Meccano's gossips. It was definitely not on – and anyway I was off girls for good.

'Well I'm not interested,' I said.

'She likes you,' he said, with a wily look. 'She thinks you're lovely.'

I was outraged. 'Lovely! Lovely!? What does she think I am – a bloody flower or something? I don't care if she thinks I'm the greatest thing on two legs. I'm off girls for good so I'm not taking her out!'

'I would if I were you,' he said, still with that wily look. 'She's got three big brothers.'

'So what?'

His reply made me feel distinctly uneasy. 'So what is that, according to Mary, Knickers *big* brothers get very annoyed if someone upsets her – like not taking her out.'

The emphasis on 'big' sounded ominous. I began to feel I was being backed into a corner.

'Look Dave,' I said belligerently, 'just whose side are you on? All this big brother stuff and ganging up with the Press Shop birds. I though you were a mate of mine.'

'I am,' he replied, suddenly serious, 'and it's all on the level. I thought you'd be chuffed to take her out – enough other fellas have tried.'

'Well I'm not other fellas,' I said, huffily. 'How would you feel if someone was trying to force you to take a bird out when you didn't want to?'

'If it was Knicker, I'd be there like a shot with my trousers over my arm,' he grinned.

I glared at him. 'Don't be bloody crude, she's a nice girl.'

'I agree with you – but I'll bet she does a turn. Anyway, if that's the way you feel, I'll tell Mary that you're not interested shall I?'

This sounded like a dodgy situation. 'Er ... let me think about it.'

It was getting late and people were beginning to drift back towards the factory entrance.

Stan glided up on his bike, beads of sweat glistening on his forehead. 'Hiya fellas.

Thought I was going to be late but my watch must be fast.'

'There's about ten minutes yet,' I said as we moved aside so he could put his bike into an empty slot.

He came and stood beside us, mopping his face with his handkerchief. 'I've just seen Andy on the back of Johno's motorbike. They were going like the clappers along Rathbone Road.'

'It's a lovely bike,' I said.

There was the sound of an engine screaming down through the gears.

Chris looked towards the gate. 'Here they come.'

The Bullet turned in at the gate and cruised slowly over to the motorbike area. Andy helped Johno to pull the machine onto its stand, his face flushed, his eyes bright with excitement. We wandered over, savouring the smell of hot metal and oil.

'That was great Ronnie,' Andy cried. 'Thanks a lot.'

Johno took a comb from his pocket and began to comb his wind-blown hair. 'Goes well doesn't it?' He turned to us. 'I'll give you guys a ride tomorrow if it's not raining.'

'Thanks Ronnie,' we chorused.

As the five minute hooter sounded, Freddie came in with a newspaper under his arm. 'Guess who Liverpool are playing in the next round of the FA Cup?'

'Russia?'

'Australia?'

'China?'

'Don't be bloody stupid,' said the Liverpool fanatic. 'It's Everton. They'll slaughter them!'

As we hurried up the corridor, with our friend crowing sickeningly about his pillion ride, I happened to look into the Press Shop. Knicker was standing by a press, looking out through the windows. Our eyes met, she smiled and raised a hand, wiggling her fingers in greeting.

To keep my options open, and making sure none of my companions saw me, I wiggled back.

We parted company at the door of the Tool Repair. Bas was off again and I'd been sent back in the grinders while he was away as there was a lot on. Grinding washers was my current job; Knicker, and what to do about her, my pressing problem. Chris had discovered that her name was Rose, which seemed much nicer than Knicker.

I thought about my dilemma as I neatly carpeted the wet grinder's big, flat magnet with dozens of washers which had to be ground to a precise thickness. The whole business was rather ironic really. The girls I had avidly pursued refused to have me at any price, whereas a girl I had no interest in, seemed prepared to be making great efforts to get me. Although I was still unsure what to do, the knowledge of Rose's personal Mafia lurking in the background, was certainly having an affect on my line of thinking. And, after all, she was very attractive, and it was quite flattering to be wooed for a change instead of being bluntly told to 'Fuck Off.' I'll bet Rose wouldn't use words like that. I made up my mind up. At tea-break I'd tell Chris to tell Mary to ask Rose if I could take her to the pictures on Saturday night.

Happy now I'd made the decision, I pressed the start button. The big wheel quickly whined up to top speed. I started the pump and as the clouds of spray began to swirl down I set the traverse in motion. Smoothly the table began to slide backwards and forwards. Slowly I wound the wheel down until, with a brief shower of sparks, it touched the bed of washers, and all hell broke loose! There was a sound like machine guns firing as the washers were catapulted off and sent ricocheting madly round the thin, steel guard surrounding the table.

For a split second I stood, paralysed by the appalling din, then I hit every stop button in sight and a merciful peace descended. The loud, derisive cheers that rose on all sides turned my shocked face to an embarrassed scarlet as I realised what I had done – or rather what I had not done. Preoccupied with my love life, I'd forgotten to turn the magnet on!

As I began picking up the washers from the dripping table a voice from behind called out cheerfully, 'That was a good one Roy – let's have another.'

A quick grin over my shoulder gave the impression that I hadn't been at all rattled by the incident, but the grin was false, and the hands picking up the washers were trembling.

Thanks to the high guard all the potential missiles, unleashed by my carelessness, had effectively been contained. I shuddered to think what carnage could have been wreaked if I had been running the machine without bothering to fit the front access panel, as I sometimes did. My dad's words echoed in my mind : 'Never forget that machines will serve you but they also have the power to maim and kill.' Well, I'd forgotten those words and paid the price but, thankfully, only my pride had been hurt!

I was still washer hunting when Bill Jackson, the foreman, strolled up. 'What happened?'

Scarlet faced again, I confessed. 'I forgot to put the magnet on.'

He tut-tutted. 'Any damage?'

'I don't think so,' I said. 'The wheel just whipped them off the magnet.'

'Are you alright?'

'Yes,' I replied, adding ruefully, 'but I think I'd better go and change my underpants.'

'Teach you not to do it again,' he said, with a faint smile, and strolled away.

I liked Bill Jackson.

It was all fixed up. Via Dave and Mary I asked Rose if I could take her too the pictures on Saturday night. Via Mary and Dave, Rose said okay, but where and what time? I suggested the Abbey Cinema in Wavertree at half past six. Rose sent back the message that she'd be there and, 'Don't be late.'

Chris was quite excited by this arrangement. 'I wouldn't mind being you, I'll bet she does a turn. Don't forget to take the necessary.'

'Aw come on,' I protested. 'I've never even spoken to her. We're only going to the pictures anyway.'

'Ah yes,' he said, with a knowing look, 'but it's what happens after the pictures that matters.'

My friend's conviction that Rose 'did a turn' rekindled my uneasy feelings concerning my Saturday night date, for although I well knew the theory of the more interesting side of life, as far as the practice was concerned I was almost a complete novice. Eyeing the talent and boasting about fictitious conquests with a crowd of friends was one thing; the prospect of spending the evening alone with a girl who could well be highly experienced in the carnal arts, was a very different kettle of fish!

If Chris was right – and I was hourly becoming more convinced that he was – I had the additional problem of obtaining the necessary.

From time to time small, green and purple, packets, with the mysterious word 'Ona' printed on them, circulated throughout the apprentice ranks. Like highly prized trophies they were quickly snapped up, to be gloatingly tucked away in the lucky owner's wallet. To us young apprentices, carrying a contraceptive gave a certain status. It proved that we weren't just all talk, but knew exactly what it was all about and were where ready for action at the first opportunity.

In reality, except for an occasional bravado airing, those little green and purple promises of manhood lay forlorn and unused until the contents perished and were consigned to the bin. But it didn't really matter, the ring impressed into the wallet's leather by the deceased french letter, preserved the desired public image until the next little package came along. The ring in my wallet had been devoid of substance for so long that it had almost faded away. Requests whispered furtively in my friends' ears were totally unproductive – their wallets suffered from the same Mother Hubbard syndrome as mine.

In Pursuit of the Necessary

'Nip up to the barber's at lunch-time,' suggested Andy, 'he sells them. You could try one on while he's giving you a haircut!'

I didn't need a haircut, but I did need the necessary, so lunch-time saw me nervously standing outside the Barber Shop on Rathbone Road.

As I sidled past the door for the third time, Andy said, exasperatedly, 'If you don't get a move on, by the time you get in there you're going to need a bloody haircut!'

'I'm going! I'm going!' I said plaintively. 'Just don't rush me that's all.' Then throwing caution to the wind, I galloped through the door.

The place was packed with waiting, smoking customers. My nerve began to crack. I shored it up and walked over to the barber. He was busily snipping away with his back to me. Self - consciously I eyed the customers. They all looked like my dad! The barber finally noticed me. 'Yes?'

I tottered out onto the pavement.

'Well?' demanded Chris. 'Did you get … ?' and that was as far as he got as he noticed what I was carrying in my hand. 'A jar of Brylcreem?' he shrieked, in disbelief. 'Andy! He's going to do it with a jar of bloody Brylcreem!'

Face aflame I hurried off round the corner into Binns Road. Passers-by glanced curiously at the two reeling, hysterical figures following in my wake.

'Ha! Ha! Ha! He's going to use a jar of bloody Brylcreem!' And so on and so on.

At any other time I would have readily joined in this frenzy of mirth, but the shock of seeing all those dad look-a-likes observing me on my furtive errand, plus the fruitless spending of cash (always in short supply), had put a severe damper on my sense of humour.

Weak with merriment, my friends subsided onto the low wall in front of the houses.

'I'm glad you thought it was so funny,' I said sarcastically, shoving the cause of all the hilarity into my pocket.

'Oh we did, we did,' they chortled.

'Can I come and watch?' sniggered Andy. 'I'd love to see how it's done with a jar of Brylcreem.'

I wasn't in the mood. 'No you bloody well can't, and for two pins I wouldn't go myself.'

Chris blew his nose violently. 'What happened?'

'The bloody place was full of older men, and they were all staring at me.'

'So what did you do?'

'I panicked like hell and asked for the first thing that came into my head.'

'Good job it wasn't a packet if razor blades,' remarked Andy, thoughtfully. 'At least you can use the Brylcreem.'

I stared at him suspiciously. 'What's that supposed to mean?'

With a patronising smile, he replied. 'Well let's face it, it'll be years before you need to use a razor.'

'What are you talking about?' I cried, indignant at this slight on my manhood. 'I had a shave this morning if you must know.'

He laughed derisively. 'Come off it. You don't need to shave – the cat could lick that bum fluff off in a couple of seconds.'

This was too much. 'Now look you bloody turd, I'm telling you I have to shave an I had a ...'

'He's only pulling your pisser,' laughed Chris, getting up from the wall. 'So what are you going to do now?'

I raised my eyes to heaven and spoke the truth. 'I'm buggered if I know!'

Cycling slowly home, I wrestled with my problem, which had now assumed huge proportions. I was so convinced that by Sunday morning my virginity would be a thing of the past, that the need to procure the necessary had reached almost life or death proportions. All the stories I had heard about ashen-faced girls whispering those fateful words: 'I'm a month late,' into a carefree boy friend's ear, thereby bringing his carefree world crashing in ruins, were busily whispering that fateful message into my ear. I was well and truly trapped, and should Saturday night arrive without that faded ring in my wallet being revitalised, I could well become the recipient of that fateful message, with three big brothers lurking in the background to enforce whatever their sister decided to do about the problem.

Despondently I cycled on. Then, suddenly, salvation! In the long line of shops bordering Picton Road my despairing eyes saw that life-saving word – Chemist. Of course! Why hadn't I thought of it before? Every chemist sold the necessary, I'd even seen packets tucked away in the corner of the window display.

Without a second thought, I bounced my bike onto the pavement, coasting up to the shop and dismounted. It was still open. As I pushed the door open an incredibly loud bell clanged through the gloomy interior, the echoes slowly dying away as I reached the counter. A tiny, elderly woman appeared through a doorway at the end of the counter, peering at me through small, rimless glasses. 'Yes?' she enquired, with a smile.

My confidence began to ebb, but I was desperate. 'A packet of contraceptives please!' I blurted out.

She looked at me vaguely, cupping a hand behind an ear. 'A what?'

My God! she was deaf! I'd have to go through it all again. 'A packet of … ' I shouted, but the doorbell drowned the rest of the sentence. It was like some awful nightmare and I must escape. 'It doesn't matter!' I bellowed, over the dying jangles, and turning wildly to flee the scene, blundered straight into a small pram parked behind me. The pram's tiny occupant immediately set up a hair-raising howl which made the doorbell sound like a whisper.

'Sorry!' I shouted to the young mother, standing calmly holding the pram's handle. She smiled resignedly and the next second I clanged through the door, intent on putting as much distance as possible between me and that dreadful shop. But the nightmare wasn't over yet.

'Just a minute,' commanded a stern voice as I shot through the door. 'I want a word with you.'

The stern voice belonged to a very large, unsmiling guardian of the law.

Bereft of speech, I stared up at the forbidding face. From his immeasurable height the figure of doom stared down at me. He pointed an accusing finger at my bike leaning against the window. 'What's the idea of riding that machine on the pavement?'

And still I stared, shocked into silence as the infant howls inside the shop rose to a crescendo.

'Well?' demanded the voice of authority. 'I haven't got all day!'

'I don't know what you're talking about!' I babbled wildly. 'I wasn't riding on the pavement,'

The figure heaved a sigh of exasperation. 'Don't give me that ... sonny. Just a few minutes ago I saw you bounce that machine,' he pointed again, 'over the kerb and ride it along the pavement.' A large hand began to unbutton his tunic pocket. 'And,' continued my persecutor relentlessly, 'if you insist on denying the fact we shall just have to take the matter further – won't we? Riding a bicycle on the footpath is breaking the law.'

At these words all my former problems suddenly paled into insignificance. My parents would go barmy if I got into trouble with the law. I swallowed hard and said humbly, 'I'm sorry officer, I wasn't thinking what I was saying. I've had a blinding headache all day and when I saw the Chemists I just had to stop and get some Aspirins.'

Halfway out of the pocket, the notebook paused.

Desperately I pressed the point home. 'Honestly officer. I've been in such pain all day that I didn't realise what I was doing. All I could think about was getting something to stop the pain.'

'And did you get any?'

'No! The lady behind the counter was deaf and then the baby started screaming and I just had to get away.'

The notebook slid back into the pocket. 'I can understand that,' said the kindly keeper of the law. 'Get headaches myself sometimes. Go on then. Gerroff home and don't do it again. And see if you can get some Aspirins on the way.'

Fervently promising to forever keep within the law in future, I pushed my bike onto the road and sprinted away.

My dog's ecstatic, tail-wagging welcome was a complete waste of energy that dreary evening. All his panting entreaties managed to elicit was a brief scratch behind the ear and a half-hearted stroke.

After a mumbled greeting to my mum and older brother, the best I could manage on a large helping of hot-pot, normally demolished in five minutes flat, was desultory fork poking until small, floating islands of congealing fat indicated that my tail-wagging friend was in for a treat.

'Are you feeling ill or something?' asked my concerned parent. 'You've hardly touched your dinner.'

'Oh I'm all right,' I answered, dolefully. 'Just a bit tired that's all. Sorry about the hot-pot, I seem to have lost my appetite.'

A hand waved dismissively. 'It doesn't matter, the dog can have it.' She picked up the plate. 'Are you sure your all right? you look very pale – perhaps you're sickening for something.'

She was dead right there. I was sickening alright, but not in the way she thought. Thank God my thoughts were my own. If my worried mother had the slightest inkling of the true reasons for my deathly complexion, she'd have a fit.

A dish of apple pie and custard suffered a similar fate to the hot-pot and roused my mother's anxiety to new heights.

'You must be ill,' she said worriedly. 'I've never known you to leave apple pie before.' An enquiring hand was laid gently on my forehead. 'You don't feel hot though.'

Irritably I shook off the solicitous hand. 'I'm fine I tell you. Just leave me alone.'

She paused uncertainly, then scored a direct hit. 'Has something happened at work to upset you?'

I felt a guilty flush stealing up my neck, but before I could answer my brother looked up from his book and, with a wide grin, announced, 'I know what it is – he's in love.'

'No I'm not!' I retorted, hotly, 'so don't you start! I'm not ill; I'm not in love, and everything's fine at work – so leave me alone!'

The welcome sound of my dad's key in the front door lock saved me from further interrogation.

By the time he'd finished his meal I'd managed to cover my worried misery with a veneer of the day's doings; with certain parts carefully edited out. For the rest of the evening I effectively avoided further cross examination by searching the wavebands on our old Raleigh wireless set, with my ear glued to the loudspeaker, to try and find the heady music of Radio Luxembourg.

Friday morning was only a day away from Saturday morning, and Saturday morning was just twenty four hours from Sunday morning, and by then I could be done for! Up the creek without a paddle! Finished! Knackered! And then, in a few short weeks my Luxembourg listening ear could receive tidings of great woe; the shotguns would be loaded, the priest or vicar primed, and my life could be over before it had even stated – and all because I couldn't find that tiny scrap of rubber.

Judging by the quantities I seen floating wraith-like down the Mersey tide – until they were shredded by the ferry boat propellers – the chemist and barber shops of Liverpool must have been bursting at the seams with the things. There were thousands to be had, just for the asking and I couldn't get hold of a miserable one because my nerve had gone and I couldn't ask again. Floating away on the tide with those pale wraiths seemed infinitely preferable to once again having to brave the horrors of the clanging, screaming baby chemists or the smoky barbers shop where all the waiting customers were spying on me.

I was almost resigned to my fate. One small glimmer of hope remained – hospital. If I was knocked off my bike on my way to work all my problems would be solved. With this in mind I weaved a very erratic course to Binns Road that drizzly Friday morning. But I was not destined to be let off the hook that way. Liverpool drivers, and particularly Liverpool Corporation bus drivers, were past masters at avoiding wobbling cyclists and all I got for my efforts were indignant horn blasts and shouted obscenities.

Chris grinned lecherously as we pushed our bikes into the racks. 'Roll on tomorrow night, eh?'

'Bugger off!' I snapped. 'I'm not in the mood.'

He kept on grinning. 'You will be tomorrow night, once you've got her knickers off – if she wears any. Have you got the necessary?'

'No I haven't, if you must know, and I wish you'd belt up about screwing her, I think she's a nice girl, and anyway I've got more important things to think about.'

His eyes widened in mock surprise. 'More important?' he echoed. 'Nothing's more important than getting your end away.'

We trailed in to the clock with Chris warming to his theme. 'Are you worried because you can't get the necessary?' he wheedled. 'Is that it?'

'Shurrup!'

Undeterred, he wheedled on. 'Well is it?'

Silence.

'Well?'

Suddenly my frayed nerves snapped and I lost my temper. It was all this smirking idiot's fault that I was in this mess in the first place - passing on messages I didn't want to hear.

Oblivious of the jostling throng around us, I rounded on him. 'Yes it bloody well is if you must know! I don't know what I'm going to do and it's all your bloody fault!'

That wiped the smirk away. He grabbed my arm. 'Surrup!' he hissed, urgently. 'You'll have the whole bloody factory finding out!'

I shook off the restraining hand. 'They'll find out soon enough if I put her up the stick because I can't get the necessary,' I said bitterly.

He laughed as we walked on. 'That's what I wanted to tell you. I know where you can get one with no problems.'

Hope! 'On the level?'

'Dead level.'

My heart lifted. 'Where?'

'Doddy.'

'Doddy!' I repeated incredulously. 'Doddy? What would he be doing with one? He's too old. I'll bet he's forgotten where it is, never mind what to do with it.'

We pushed our way to the clock, reaching it just as Rose was passing. She stopped in a cloud of perfume and our eyes met. She smiled, 'Hiya.'

I swallowed. 'Hiya.'

Chris jabbed me conspiratorially in the back.

'All right for tomorrow night?' she asked.

I swallowed again. 'I'll be there.'

'See you then. Don't be late.' And she wafted away with the crowd.

We punched our numbers. The hooter wailed urgently. Strolling along the passage I said, incredulously, 'Did you hear that?'

'Don't be late,' he mimicked, knocking me in the ribs with his elbow. 'She must be keen eh? You lucky bugger. She looked a cracker this morning.'

I'd thought so too. 'She did, didn't she.'

We passed the cloak rooms, we had taken to putting our

coats in our workshop lockers, and turned the corner into the corridor.

'Look Chris,' I said seriously. 'Is this really on the level about Doddy, because I'll tell you now, if I can't get one I'm not bloody well turning up and I don't care if she's got twenty bloody brothers!'

We passed the Toolstores with a strident – 'Morning Bill!' sung through the open hatch. A faint, 'Morning' drifted along behind us as Chris said, 'It is on the level honest. I'll tell you at tea-break.'

Feeling that the dark clouds which had been hanging over me for days were beginning to float away, I slid open the door to the Tool Repair, and although the sight of Bill Jackson looking pointedly at his watch injected instant acceleration into my progress, those clouds continued to melt away. But not for long; authority saw to that.

I hurriedly 'Morning'd' my workmates as I sped by to the end of the shop, hurriedly changed into my overall and hurriedly began setting up the large milling cutter I had to sharpen on the cutter grinder. So far so good. I wound the wheel head up, sighting along the cutter's teeth for the correct angle, simultaneously watching my foreman's reflection in the Hardening Shop windows. He was still in his office and appeared to be talking on the phone. I heaved a sigh of relief, the pointed watch scrutinising was obviously not going any further.. Life was looking rosy again, but the reflection of a white-coated figure striding purposely towards me along the aisle between the grinders, brought the clouds back blacker than ever.

By the time the foreman reached me I had that awful, sinking, 'I'm in for a right bollocking' feeling in the pit of my stomach – and I was right.

With his normally placid features set dark with irritation he snapped 'Come in the office!' then, turning on his heel, he strode back along the aisle.

Despondently I pressed the stop button and even more despondently, trudged in his wake. Sniggers and chuckles marked my progress; the whole world joined in when a young apprentice was in for a bollocking. Sam Brown gave some moral support as I passed his grinder. 'You're in for it!' he chuckled.

'Close the door!'

Nervously I obeyed, hearing the friendly sounds of normality fade into the pregnant silence of impending doom.

Taking a deep breath through white, flared nostrils the foreman gave me a broadside. 'I've just had a phone call about you from Mister Simpson, who had just had a phone call, also about you and your strolling friend next door, from our Managing Director – Mister Hunter!'

I swallowed hard. Sydney Hunter wasn't the type to ring up and wish his workers a bright good morning. If you were singled out by him the result was usually a king sized bollocking – or worse. I was well and truly in the cart this time.

The phone rang. I waited in silence as it was answered. The faint sound of a voice raised in song permeated through the office windows. The tune was *Unchained Melody*, one of my Luxembourg favourites, with all my heart I wished I'd been the one out there singing it.

The phone was retuned to it's cradle. The foreman leaned back in his chair and fixed me with a cold stare. 'Have you any idea why you should be the object of so much interest to the Managing Director, so early in the morning?'

I had, but experience had taught me to me to keep my mouth shut and play the innocent in such situations. Dumbly

I shook my head. The foreman wasn't fooled for a minute.

'Don't give me that!' he expostulated. 'You know damn well what this is all about – strolling in at five past eight when you'd already clocked on! In case it has slipped your memory you're supposed to *begin* work at eight o'clock and that means be in here, not strolling along the passage yapping to your mate. This morning, unfortunately for you, Mister Hunter came in early and decided to have a walk round the factory, and what should he see on his tour? Two apprentices ambling along at five past eight as if they had all the time in the world. Well let me tell you – you haven't! In future be in here, or wherever you're working by eight o'clock. Got it!'

'Yes.' I answered meekly, privately thinking how I could boast about this bollocking to my friends.

'And I'll tell you another thing,' he continued, relentlessly. 'Mister Hunter was so annoyed that he was going to suspend you both for a week.'

I gasped, feeling the colour drain from my face. Suspension went on your record and was one step away from the sack. If the foreman had intended to scare me he'd hit the jackpot.

'But ... but ... ' I floundered.

'It's all right,' he interrupted, 'stop panicking. Mister Simpson talked him out of it.'

'Oh thanks,' I gasped, gratefully. 'It won't happen again – honestly.'

A faint smile. 'I'll believe that when I see it. But next time you might not be so lucky – so keep your nose clean.'

'I will,' I promised, fervently – and meant it, at the time.

'Okay, bollocking over, you can get back to your work. And by the way, there's two planer blades for the Woodworking Shop that need sharpening on the top bench, grind them after you've finished that cutter – and don't forget to put the magnet on this time.'

Gratefully I fled back to the noisy normality outside.

An air of gloom hung over our tea-break that morning. Chris had fared even worse than me in the bollocking stakes. Sinbad, receiving the full force of Sydney Hunter's wrath, had lost no time in passing it on, with interest.

'Told me next time I stepped out of line he'd suspend me himself – the bastard!' complained Chris, bitterly. 'Bloody Sid Hunter, snooping about. Why can't the bastard be like old Bearsley? We never had this sort of thing when he was the boss, you hardly ever saw the old fart.'

We all murmured agreement, wondering if this was some sort of purge against us, using the dreaded suspension to make us toe the line.

Freddie voiced our thoughts. 'It'll be dead miserable if they start this bloody caper every time we step out of line. We'll be too frightened to chat the talent up in case Sid Hunter's hiding round the bloody corner waiting to jump out shouting, 'Gerrout! You're suspended you dirty little bugger!'

Sniggers greeted this remark and the gloom began to lift as we wielded the ultimate weapon of ridicule, to even the score in our long running battle with authority.

'Just imagine!' cried Andy, waving his mug, 'sliding up behind a bit of crumpet, tweaking her arse and whispering, 'How about it under the conveyer, gorgeous? and when she turned round it was Sid Hunter in disguise, shouting, 'Gerrout! You're suspended you dirty little bugger!'

And we rocked and howled with laughter.

'And he'd have falsies on.' I shouted. 'Stuffed with old socks!'

'And his hair in curlers like ferret face!' roared Chris.

'And what about stockings and suspenders?' spluttered

Freddie. 'and knickers – those long, woolly ones, and he'd have to pull them down for a ... '

'Now you're getting dirty,' we cried. 'Gerrout! You're suspended you dirty little bugger!'

In my excited rocking my stool went over backwards, but I felt no pain in the heat of our verbal rebellion, and lay limply giggling as my comrades laughter reached almost hysterical heights.

An apple core landed in our midst. 'Shurrup!' shouted a voice. 'I can't read my paper with you lot giggling like a bunch of big tarts!'

Which immediately prompted a reckless chorus of loud raspberries and vigorous V signs in the complainants direction.

The rebellion died with the hooter's raucous summons, and almost before the echoes had dwindled mournfully away, the tea-break rebels all had their heads down, working hard.

It was only as I was setting up the planer blades on the wet grinder that I remembered I hadn't asked Chris about Doddy and the necessary. That brought the dark clouds billowing back. It was essential to find out what it was all about as soon as possible, which meant talking to Chris, but how could I contact him? After what had happened, nipping into the Toolroom for a quick chat would be verging on suicide. If Sinbad saw us nattering together we'd be suspended so fast our feet wouldn't touch the ground. So what was I to do to solve yet another problem in my problem-beset love life?

I was thoroughly fed up with the whole, wretched business. I'd had sleepless nights; been embarrassed to the point of mortification; fallen foul of the law and come within a hair's breadth of being suspended – not to mention being made the butt of all the Brylcreem jokes in creation – and all so I could take a girl to the pictures on Saturday night. But I was in too deep now and that Saturday rendezvous had to be kept come hell or high water, with or without the necessary – but preferably with.

By standing near one end of the grinder I could just see Chris on his milling machine through one of the arches. Unfortunately my arms were about a foot too short to operate the machine from this position. I overcame the problem by adopting a sort of rocking motion in time with the machine's long backwards and forwards traverse. Each forward motion – wind a cut on; each backward – take a look through the arch, at the back of Chris's head which, after ten frustrating minutes, became the back of Chris's stupid head! Then he happened to look round as I rocked into view. 'Bog!' I mouthed, jerking my head towards the main corridor. The next rock received an 'understood' thumbs-up and I was able to revert to operating the machine in a more normal manner.

'What's all the panic about?' asked my friend, as we settled ourselves on the wash basins. 'And make it snappy after what happened this morning – and Sid Hunter might be in one of those bogs.'

I sniggered. 'If he is I hope the bastard falls down the hole. Anyway, I've got to know about Doddy and the goodies.'

He grinned, and fumbling in his pocket, produced a packet of Woodbines and a box of matches. 'Might as well have a fag while we're talking.'

I stared. 'When did you start smoking?'

'Oh, a couple of weeks ago,' he replied, airily. 'It doesn't half impress the birds.'

Sticking a cigarette self-consciously between his lips he struck a match, inhaled deeply and immediately went into violent paroxysms of eye-watering coughing.

Startled, I banged the shaking back until the fit began to subside.

'Alright! Alright!' croaked the budding smoker, feebly pushing my hand away. 'That's enough, what are you trying to do – fracture my spine?'

'Only trying to help,' I said – then added sarcastically, 'and if that's what you have to do to impress the birds I don't think I'll bother.'

Chris looked at the small cigarette with distaste and nicked it out. 'It's these bloody Woodbines, I've had Craven A before but I couldn't afford them this week, and I don't usually inhale either.' He coughed again. 'God! that was bloody awful.'

'I don't think I'll bother,' I repeated. 'I can't afford it and they say once you start you can't stop. My dad reckons it's a mugs game.'

He blew his nose violently. 'Does your dad smoke?'

'Yeh, that's why he says it's a mugs game.'

'Mine too. but it doesn't half impress the girls and it makes you feel a bit like Humphrey Bogart.' He went into a Bogart impression. 'Frankly my dear, I don't give a damn.'

'That was Clark Gable you bloody idiot.'

A toilet flushed, the door banged open and Jimmy Whitehouse appeared, folding a newspaper. 'Hello, hello, hello, what's this? A cosy union meeting? Or are you deciding where to go when you're suspended?'

We glowered, wondering how he found out.

He laughed good naturedly, tucking the paper into the waistband of his trousers. 'Don't let it worry you. When I was an apprentice I lost count of the number of times they threatened me with suspension, but they never did – it's all talk.' He buttoned up his overall, rinsed his hands and went out.

'The bloody liar!' snorted Chris. 'He's trying to act the big shot. I'll bet he didn't say boo when he was an apprentice.'

The talk of suspension had made me nervous. 'Never mind him, tell me about Doddy. We'll have to get back or we'll be in trouble again.'

'You're right,' he said, making for the door. I'll tell you at lunch time.'

I followed him after a couple of minutes, so we'd arrive back at different times.

I was at Chris's milling machine almost before the hooter had run out of wail, to get the story.

'Well,' began Chris, 'last night, just before knocking off time, I was having a look at the die Doddy's slotting for the Centurion Tank base – have you seen the trial casting on Joe's bench; it's a real big bugger— '

'Bugger the casting!' I interrupted fiercely. 'I'll see it at some other time, get on with the story.'

He continued. 'Anyway, Doddy opened his cabinet drawer to put his vernier away and what should I see lurking there but an Ona packet. 'Aye, aye Fred,' I said, 'what's this? I thought you were past it?' Expecting him to be dead embarrassed ... '

'And was he?'

'No,' he just grinned and said, 'Oh, keep those for you young lads so you don't get into trouble. 'If you need the necessary, just come and see Fred.'

This sounded too good to be true. 'You wouldn't kid me about this Chris?'

He sighed, extending his hands, palms uppermost. 'God's truth, it's on the level – what more can I say.'

And I was convinced. 'Thanks Chris, you're a good mate. I'll go and see him at lunch time.'

Doddy was settling himself comfortably in his chair, a *Daily Herald* and a box of sandwiches lying on the slotter's circular table.

'Hiya Fred,' I began, feeling an embarrassed flush beginning.

He looked up, opening his tin of sandwiches. The strong aroma of onions filled the air.

'Hello young Roy,' he replied, lifting a sandwich and taking a large bite.

I stood uncertainly, not quite knowing what to say next.

'What are you after?' he asked, through his chewing.

'Chris said you could let me have the necessary!' I blurted out. 'I've got to have one for tomorrow night.'

He grinned and continued munching, tapping the toes of his shiny, black boots up and down on the floor as if thinking about something. Another large bite preceded, 'Come and see me later and I'll fix you up.'

Utter relief. 'Thanks Fred. Will tea-break be alright?'

He nodded, picking up the newspaper. 'That'll be okay.'

I walked on air on our lunch-time stroll and whistled my way through the afternoon to tea-break, when I presented myself at the slotter. True to his word, Fred had the precious green and purple packet waiting.

'Thanks Fred,' I said gratefully. 'How much do I owe you?'

Grinning, he waved a hand. 'You can have that. We have to look after you randy young lads. Don't want you getting into trouble do we?'

I grinned back, feeling slightly foolish. 'Er no. But thanks a lot Fred, you've really taken a load off my mind.'

Still grinning – or was it leering – my benefactor responded. 'Well the best of luck, and don't forget to let me know how you got on.'

'Oh... er... sure,' I replied, feeling a little uneasy about this request. What was he up to? Was I expected to recount all the lurid details (if there were any) of my Saturday night adventure or what? Well I'd cross that bridge when I came to it, the main thing was that the fading ring in my wallet was about to be gloriously revitalised.

As I joined the lads in our corner, Chris's enquiring glance was given a happy thumbs up.

Now I was kitted out, I began to look forward with growing confidence to Saturday night. Rose had better watch out if I got her on the back row – and that would just be the start. Later, in some secluded little nook, she'd really discover why the Toolroom apprentices had such a randy reputation.

Saturday morning was spent cleaning and overhauling my bike, and as I tinkered and adjusted and polished, my feelings seesawed wildly between excitement at the forthcoming date and black despair lest, if we did end up in some dark, secluded nook, I should be found wanting.

As the day progressed, the excitement dwindled and something approaching panic set in, which even a periodic, reassuring peep at my small packet failed to dispel. If anything those furtive peeps made the matter even worse, serving to remind me that the world of giggling, fumbling gropes was over – I was poised for a torrid entry into the big league.

Lunch-time egg and chips stuck in my throat, but for the sake of my mum's peace of mind, I persevered , managing to finish most of the meal. Later, sitting on the back step, I stroked my canine friend's furry head as my spirits sank lower and lower. Dogs had the best life. Out for walks; chasing sticks, and having their ears scratched. Not for them the frantic hunt for the necessary with the threat of three big brothers lurking round the corner. Lucky dogs simply waylaid a passing lady dog and climbed aboard for a piggy-back. Then, feeling in desperate need of reassuring male company, I biked over to some friends in Hunts Cross, a mile away. In a syndicate they had bought a 1932 BSA 350 cc. motor bike for thirty bob. There was no front mudguard, no exhaust and very little seat but the thing went like a bomb, and, for a few hours I was able to lose my problems in a reckless world of oil and petrol and ear-shattering noise. But it was only a brief respite because all the time, as I raced round that green, flat meadow, my doom was marching ever nearer.

I had said nothing of my date to my grimy, petrol-reeking friends, but as I reluctantly mounted my bike to leave, Dave shouted, above the flat note of the engine ticking over.

'Where are you off to then?'

'Got a date!' I shouted gloomily.

Standing astride the bike he made thrusting movements with his pelvis, shouting: 'Let us know how you got on. Ta-rah!' The engine noise rose to a crescendo and, with Eric sitting on the mudguard pillion, they careered off across the field.

Enviously I watched them go, then began my despondent journey home. As I pedalled slowly along, Dave's parting words came back in an echo of Doddy. 'Let's know how you got on.'

It seemed that the whole world was avidly interested in the outcome of my Saturday night assignation. The one person who viewed the prospect without any enthusiasm – was me.

Under my mother's watchful eyes I managed to give my dinner a repeat performance of lunch – just. Then it was time to get ready. I was frequently out in the evening, with my friends and usually left with a casual, 'See you later,' as I went through the front door, but tonight, when I could soon be taking a gigantic leap into manhood, such a casual leave-taking seemed wholly inadequate. 'I'm going out tonight,' I informed my family. No response. I tried again – loudly. 'I said, 'I'm going out tonight.'

This time there was some response. My dad glanced at me curiously through the smoke from his cigarette, my mum, preoccupied with her knitting, murmured, 'Don't be too late,' and my brother, looking up from the *Liverpool Echo,* said, 'So am I and don't be too long in the bathroom.'

Without being more explicit I had to be content with these small offerings, and reading into that glance from my dad that he had a shrewd idea of what I was up too, I left it at that.

As I drew the razor inexpertly across my already smooth and shining chin, a vague suspicion, which had been lurking at the back of my mind, suddenly surfaced. Old Doddy had been a bit too obliging; a bit too helpful. Why hadn't he let me pay him for the necessary? It wasn't like him to dish out charity. And then there was that queer business on Friday afternoon. Every time I happened to glance over towards the Toolroom, Doddy's grinning face would be peering in at me through one of the arches, and when he realised I'd seen him he'd wave merrily and called, 'The best of luck.'

Beyond being slightly puzzled I had paid little attention to this pantomime. Doddy often went a bit eccentric but, putting all the pieces together, that on-going excitement could well have resulted from something far more sinister than mere eccentricity, like – I quavered at the thought – that much talked-about dreaded, leaking pin hole!

Yes. That could be it. In one of his queerer moods Doddy could well think that dropping someone in the cart that way was a huge joke. With my meal turning to lead in my stomach, I fumbled feverishly for that precious packet. Dithering fingers located the contents and gently drew out the neatly rolled ring of rubber. I exhaled slowly with relief, everything seemed to be in order so far, now to check – but wait a minute! This pale circle nestling so snugly in the palm of my hand looked awfully small – much too small. What on earth was going on? Had they started making the things in different sizes? No, that would be ridiculous, but why did it look so small? Throwing caution to the winds I unrolled the tube to its full extent, and then I realised the reason for all Doddy's hilarity. Dangling, almost mockingly, from my nerveless fingers was a tiny rubber finger stall! Vitality drained away and I had to sit down on the edge of the bath, and, as I sat in a state of shock at this dirtiest of dirty tricks, another realisation struck me – it was now too late to do anything about it! At the eleventh hour my lifeline had been snatched away by a strawberry–nosed, truss–wearing old bugger with a warped sense of humour. In the desolation surrounding me I could almost hear those shotguns being loaded up again.

For a long time I sat, almost weeping with self-pity at my plight, and all the time my mind was searching frantically for an escape route – but there was none. Every exit was guarded by a burly, doting brother.

Then, suddenly, the funny side of the affair hoisted me out of my pit of despair with bewildering speed. What on earth had I been up to? All that worrying; all the sleepless nights; all the frenzied attempts to find the necessary – and for what? So I could take a girl out for an evening at the pictures. What a clown I was! If the film world ever got wind of my antics, Dean Martin and Jerry Lewis had better watch out – they could be out of a job.

And even supposing Rose was experienced and harboured carnal intentions towards my virginity, (and I only had Chris's opinion about that), she was hardly likely to try and drag me down the nearest entry for a spot of ravishing if I wasn't a willing party was she? So balls to the necessary, I could do without it.

A loud thumping on the bathroom door terminated my reverie.

'Are you going to be in there all night?' came my brother's exasperated voice. 'I've got to be out in half an hour.'

Startled, I looked at my watch. My God! I only had fifteen minutes to catch the bus!

'And about ... ' began my brother, as the door slammed open.

But I was gone and by the time he'd finished the sentence I was halfway into my suit and looking for my best shoes. Not in the wardrobe. Under the bed? No. Under my brothers bed? No. Distracted scuttling about, racing the seconds. Shoes! Shoes! Where were those bloody shoes? Get help. 'Mum!'

'Yes?' faintly.

Desperately trying to manage a Windsor knot in my tie. 'Have you seen my suede shoes?'

Silence.

Full volume. 'I said, have you seen my suede shoed?'

'They're down here under the sideboard. They're dirty.'

'Could you give them a quick brush for me please?' Where were my cuff links? Where were those bloody cuff links? 'Mum! Have you seen my – oh it's okay, I've found them.'

Grab my coat, down the stairs like a whirlwind and on with the shoes.

'Thanks mum. I've got to catch the six o'clock bus – I'm going to the Abbey. Bye!

Halfway out of the front door and a sudden thought. A quick listen – sounds of splashing in the bathroom. Up the stairs, quietly, two at a time and into the bedroom for a lightning raid on my brother's much prized bottle of Old Spice aftershave. Then away triumphantly to catch the bus.

I arrived at the bus stop with only seconds to spare before the big, green double-decker appeared. Feverishly I flagged it down. The driver must have been in a good mood for the bus ground to a halt a mere twenty yards passed the stop, and knowing, from past experience, that I only had a few seconds before the starting bell was rung, I sprinted after it.

'Thanks for stopping!' I panted sarcastically, as I leaped onto the platform.

Ignoring that remark, the small conductor demanded, 'Wer yer goin?'

'Wavertree – the Abbey,' I puffed, staggering back as the bus lurched forward.

Legs wide apart to counter his driver's racing start, the conductor wound the handle on his ticket machine and, fixing me with an unfriendly eye, he ripped the ticket off and thrust it towards me. 'Four-pence.'

He sniffed the air critically through his untidy, ginger moustache as I fumbled for the money. 'Smells like someone's wearin his mam's scent,' he observed knowingly to the rest of the bus.

Bloody cheek! 'If you must know,' I snapped, staring up the stairs, 'it's dead expensive aftershave.'

More loud sniffing, 'Well it smells like scent.' floated up after me.'

I spent most of the journey, through Penny Lane to the Abbey, trying to think up clever remarks to fling at that uniformed smart Alec as I got off the bus, but only managed a shouted, 'And I hope your bus breaks down!' at the back of the retreating vehicle.

But ginger moustache had the last word. Leaning out precariously as the bus swayed round the corner he shouted derisively, 'An yer still smell like a big pansy!'

I crossed the road beginning to regret that lightning raid on the Old Spice.

In the light streaming through the windows of the huge, curved front of the cinema, I could see people bustling across the wide pavement and into the foyer. Here and there other figures stood, waiting for their dates or friends. A surreptitious tour of these solitary shadows established that Rose wasn't among them, so I joined their silent ranks.

The minutes ticked away. From time to time a lucky shadow was joined by a new arrival and the lonely vigil was over as the chattering couple hurried in to the brightly lit foyer. More lucky shadows – more couples, and still I waited. There were few of us left now. I turned my collar up against the cold breeze and looked at the time. Had I only been here for fifteen minutes? It felt like hours. Was she never going to come? And then the unthinkable crept stealthily into my mind. Suppose she didn't come at all? Or even worse, she'd never intended to come in the first place and this date had been cooked up to give the girls in the Press Shop a good laugh at my expense. I'd heard of that rotten trick being played before. I shivered at the thought and had a quick look round, half expecting to see a crowd of giggling females watching my every move – but of course there was nothing. Reassured, and feeling a bit sheepish at my sudden panic, I resumed my vigil, certain that Rose would come.

But dark and windswept pavements are Doubt's domain and as the time crept by, and my feet grew colder, I became more and more convinced that I waited in vain. It was strange, a few short hours ago I would have heaved a great sigh of relief at this prospect, but now, for some unaccountable reason, I desperately hoped that Rose would come.

Thrusting my hands deeper into my pockets I gloomily

surveyed the almost deserted scene for the fiftieth time. A dark figure was hurrying towards me, her high heels tapping loudly on the pavement. It was Rose. She'd come after all. Gloom fell away like a discarded cloak as I stepped forward to meet her, but at the last moment she turned aside and greeted a nearby figure with a quick hug. 'Sorry I'm late Kenny,' I heard her say. 'But we had a rush on and I had to work over.' Bending his head her boyfriend whispered something in her ear that made her laugh and linking arms they strolled away.

Despondently I watched them stop at the sweet kiosk – a lucky couple going to the pictures on a Saturday night.

A look at my watch told me it was a quarter to seven, then the decision. If she wasn't here by seven o'clock she'd had it! I was off! But off where? Home I suppose, there was little point in calling on any of my friends – they'd all be out enjoying themselves somewhere – the lucky buggers. Why wasn't I part of that laughing crowd instead of standing here on my own, cold and miserable and quite obviously stood up? Bloody girls! Every time I got involved with one I ended up insulted and upset. Well, after this fiasco I'd really finished with them. Just let those eyelashes start fluttering seductively in my direction and hear the insults fly. For two pins I'd bugger off right now, never mind waiting until seven o'clock. But no! I'd decided to stay until seven so I would stay until seven – but not one second longer. God, my feet are cold with this standing, a little walk round the corner and back might help to warm them up and relieve the monotony.

As I wandered off, the glare of headlights swept round the across the forecourt as yet another bus roared round the corner and squealed to a stop. I remembered ginger moustache. Where was he now? With a bit of luck, in hospital after falling off his bus shouting insulting remarks at law abiding passengers, and serve him bloody well right. Did I really smell like a pansy? Well it didn't matter either way, now I'd been stood up. Then the sharp skittering of heels on the pavement and a girl's voice calling urgently 'Roy! Wait!' It was Rose.

I stopped abruptly and turned to meet her. As she hurried towards me I tried to think of some appropriate greeting but all that emerged was a feeble 'Oh hello.'

'I thought you were goin' in without me,' she said, slightly breathless with rushing. 'I'm awful sorry I'm late … I washed my hair an' couldn't get it to dry … and I missed the bus an' the next one was full … an' I had to wait for the next one an' as we came round the corner I saw you walkin' away and I thought I'd missed you.' She smiled in the cinema lights and said simply, 'but I hadn't.' Then she put her arms around me and whispered, 'Thanks so much for waiting, I'll make it up to you I promise.'

Mt heart skipped a beat. Did she mean what I thought she meant?

And suddenly I felt an overwhelming affection for this lovely girl who, unknowingly had been the cause of so much trauma in my life. I wanted to put my arms around her and whisper 'I love you,' but I didn't because I'd never done that before and didn't have the nerve to do it now. So I said, as warmly as I could, 'Well, I'm so glad you finally came, shall we go in?'

At the door there was just one of my waiting companions still waiting, grinding the remains of his cigarette under a venomous heel. He had my sympathy. I could afford that luxury now that my own lonely vigil was over.

And then we were in that warm, scented, smoky darkness, shuffling apologetically along the row of knees to the two empty seats picked out by the thin beam of the usherette's torch. Voices boomed and the music soared as the black and white shapes of the 'B' picture pranced across the screen. A cloud of heady perfume enveloped me as Rose leaned over and whispered, 'What's this filum called?'

'I don't know,' I whispered back. 'I forgot to look.'

With a faint 'Oh' she settled back in her seat.

A few minutes later the perfume wafted in again. 'What's the big picture called then?'

I knew this one. '*The War of the Worlds.*'

'Oh.' Then. 'Have you seen it before?'

'No.'

'Oh.'

An irritated '*Shhhush!*' from behind brought our whispered conversation to an abrupt end.

The 'B' film (whatever it was called), continued its noisy, flickering progress. The sleeve of Rose's coat brushed against my hand as she offered an open packet of cigarettes. I hesitated. I'd never tried smoking. The contented puffing on a cigarette had always seemed far away in adulthood, but tonight was special. I was suddenly growing up, so why not? With a whispered 'Thanks,' and the excuse, 'I've forgotten mine.' I took one.

Her lighter clicked, the tiny flame glowing warm and intimate as she held it towards me. Naively I sucked, drawing in a stream of acrid smoke that burned my throat, rushed up my nose and made my eyes water. I seemed to be enveloped by a dense cloud as I struggled for breath and fought an overwhelming urge to cough and cough and cough.

Gradually the urge subsided, and slowly, almost reluctantly, my smoke cloud spiralled upwards, taking with it all my short-lived aspirations to become a smoker. But what could I do with the unwanted cigarette? I couldn't very well stub it out in the ashtray after just one puff, that might be noticed, and I certainly wasn't going to risk another drag on the awful thing. The best way seemed to be to just let it burn away until I could get rid of it in the ashtray. That cigarette seemed to burn for ever and no matter where I held it a fickle draught kept drifting the smoke up my nose and into my watering eyes.

The film (whatever it was called) ended, the lights came on and a babble of voices rose around us. Leaning forward Rose began to struggle out of her coat. Gallantly I tried to help, somehow getting my fingers tangled in her hair.

'Ouch!' she yelped – then laughing, 'Don't pull it all out.'

'Sorry!' I apologised, crimson faced with embarrassment.

Expertly she patted the disturbed curls into place and opened her handbag. 'Would you like another ciggy?'

Panic! I couldn't go through all that again – especially now the lights were on. I looked for salvation and found it in the tray–carrying girl walking down the steps to the front of the circle.

'Let's have an ice-cream.' I suggested, enthusiastically. And to my relief the packet of doom was returned to its lair amongst the lipsticks and powder compacts.

She had a lovely smile. 'Thanks. I'll have a tub – raspberry ripple.'

I squeezed my way past fewer knees and feet and joined the queue. As I waited I looked idly at the sea of faces surrounding me, people were talking, laughing, smoking and eating ice cream. Everyone was enjoying themselves except me – and probably Rose. Up to now the evening had not exactly been and outstanding success, I could only hope it would get better.

'Yes?' The ice cream girl's voice broke in to my thoughts.

'Two raspberry ripple tubs, please.'

'No raspberry, only vanilla.'

'Okay. Two vanilla tubs, then.' I said, handing over my last pound note.

She sighed. 'Haven't you got any less? I'm almost out of change. Everyone's been givin' me pound notes tonight.'

I hastily fumbled in my pocket, dropped half a crown on the floor and had to hunt around by the girl's legs to find it, whilst the rest of the queue waited patiently. As I got up a wit behind me offered, 'It's not your night mate.' I hoped he was wrong.

Rose was smiling as I walked back up the steps, her red hair almost startlingly bright above the ocelot pattern of the coat draped over her shoulders. Was that an affectionate – here comes my lovely boyfriend – smile? Or a derisive laugh initiated by my grovelling antics in front of the ice cream queue? I felt I needed to know.

'Sorry, she only had vanilla.' I said, sitting down.

'It's alright, and thanks.' She peeled off the lid. 'I saw you looking about on the floor, what happened?'

I peeled off my own lid. 'I dropped half a dollar on the floor and had to grovel about to find it again.'

She looked concerned. 'Poor you. Were you dead embarrassed in front of all them people?'

'Nah. It was a bit of a laugh really,' I boasted, relieved to discover that whatever it was she'd been smiling about it hadn't been me.

I really enjoyed that ice cream. It was so soothing after my disastrous foray into the smoker's world that I almost forgot Rose was there as I happily carved away with my little wooden spoon.

The lights began to dim; the music faded away; Rose dropped her empty tub with a hollow clack.

'Do you like these sort of filums?' she asked.

I dropped my tub with a hollow clack. 'What sort of films?'

'You know. Like this *War of the Worlds*, fightin' and that sort of thing.'

I thought for a moment. 'I dunno. Not a lot I suppose. I like a good comedy really.'

'Me too!' she said enthusiastically. 'Dean Martin and Jerry Lewis have me in fits.'

On the screen the Pathe News cockerel was crowing loudly, but not loud enough to drown the sharp click of a handbag being opened. The dreaded packet appeared. 'Would you like one?'

Desperation gave me inspiration. 'No thanks, I've packed it in.'

'Oh. But you had one before.'

'I know, but I'd packed it in really.'

'Oh.' A pause. 'You don't mind if I do?'

'No. You go ahead, it's ... '

'*Shhhhsh*' from close behind again effectively curtailed any further conversation.

The news ended; *The War of the Worlds* began and Rose snuggled closer. The heat ray incinerating three men induced a horrified gasp and a small, warm hand clutching mine. I clutched back.

And that was how we stayed for the rest of the film. The irritated shusher behind us had dealt my courage a mortal blow, effectively putting paid to any attempt at more intimate contact. Like loyal subjects we stood for the National Anthem, then joined hundreds of other loyal subjects thronging towards the exits.

'Did you like the picture?' I asked, as we clattered down the stairs.

Rose pulled up her collar against the cold air wafting in

through the doorway. 'It was alright I suppose. I mean those machines an death rays an' things were clever, an' the Martians were really slimy – they gave me the creeps. Ugh!' She shivered, holding her collar up tightly as she surveyed the dark sky. 'Do you think there really could be monsters like that on Mars, plannin' to come down here?'

I sniggered disdainfully. 'Nah. I don't suppose there's anything on Mars, never mind green things with three eyes. And even if there was and they landed here they'd all end up working at Meccano.'

She giggled. But, despite my light hearted words, I found my own eyes drawn irresistibly to that mysterious and suddenly menacing void above the street lamps.

We caught a bus to Penny Lane and another up Smithdown Road, where we got off.

Rose guided me down a shadowy gas-lit street.

'My gran lives somewhere near here,' I said. 'In Greenleaf Street.'

'That's further down on the other side,' my guide informed me. 'What's her name?'

'Mrs. Murphy.'

She giggled. 'There's millions of Mrs. Murphy's round here.'

We walked on, talking, and somewhere along the way we started holding hands. Then thoughts came sneaking stealthily into my mind – carnal thoughts. Sternly I pushed them out. Temptation had no place when all the goodies were locked away in the dark and shuttered Chemist shops.

Rose stopped by a narrow entry that ran between the terraced houses and pointed up the street. 'I live just up there.'

'Oh. I see,' I said, suddenly aware of my heart beating. 'Well

... er ... thanks for coming, I enjoyed it. P'raps we can go out again sometime. I'll ... er see you in work then.'

She pulled me gently into the dark passage. 'Aren't you goin' to kiss me goodnight?' she asked, softly.

I swallowed. My heart thumped almost painfully in my ears. 'Well ... er ... yes – if you don't mind.'

Reaching up she linked her hands behind my neck and pulled gently. 'I don't mind,' she whispered.

Her perfume enveloped me like a seductive cloak as her warm, soft lips clung to mine and our bodies seemed to mould together. My senses reeled with excitement as the world contracted into a warm, vibrant moment of ecstasy. I'd never experienced anything remotely like it, and if all the Martians in creation had suddenly landed in the street outside I wouldn't even have noticed.

If Mary was like an eel – Rose was a boa constrictor. In that dark entry of smoke–stained bricks we writhed together like two souls in torment. My virginity was going for a Burton tonight and I couldn't have cared less about the necessary.

My hand slid into her coat and under her sweater and our writhing became a wrestling match.

'Oh Roy!' She gasped, as my newly-awakened passion took control, and we kissed and struggled, and held each other until my hand went under her brassiere and gained the warm, soft breast with the nipple proud and erect.

And then I felt her hand sliding down between us until it reached the buttons of the very centre of my desire – and it was all over! I was standing in a cold, draughty entry with legs like two pieces of wet string, holding a moaning, passionate girl I hardly even knew!

'I ... I'd better go,' I gasped. 'I'll miss the bus.'

Rose responded with a vicious half Nelson round my neck.

'Bugger the bus!' and her mouth clamped so tightly over mine that I could hardly breath.

Panicking now, I tore myself free. 'Honest Rose, I'll have to go!' I gabbled. 'If I miss the bus I'll have to walk, and it's miles and miles home.'

The grip relaxed and she giggled. 'Okay. We couldn't have you walking home in that state could we? You'd never make it!'

I blushed furiously in the darkness. She knew; and before long everyone in the Press Shop would know, and then it was only a short step before the Toolroom knew, and my life would be made a misery of taunting remarks and smart dirty jokes.

The dim light filtering in from the street was suddenly blocked out by a vast, black shape.

I fought an overwhelming urge to run as something advanced slowly along the entry.

'That you Rose?' enquired a gruff voice.

'Yes Eric.'

The shape spoke again. 'Everythin' awright?'

I poised myself for flight.

'Yes Eric,' said Rose, again. 'I'm just sayin' goodnight to my friend.'

'Okay,' said Eric, 'but mam sez you're to come in now, it's late.'

'Be in in a minute,' said my saviour, and, apparently satisfied, the dark shape slowly retreated.

I felt the sweat on my forehead growing cold in the night air and thanked my lucky stars that I'd been unable to consummate our brief relationship. If that hulking great shadow had caught me humping his beloved sister, I wouldn't have had to pay for the bus home – what was left of me would have got a free ride to Sefton General Hospital.

We kissed goodbye; a gentle, understanding – almost I love you – kiss and walked our separate ways. As I hurried along on legs still dithering from that awakening moment, the sharp tap of Rose's heels came echoing back down the street. Then silence, the slam of a door and it was all a scented memory.

Feeling depressed and miserable, I made my way back to Smithdown Road and huddled in a shop doorway, near the bus stop, so I was out of the cold wind, and my thoughts were gloomy. What with one thing and another the evening hadn't been much of a success, and the end had been verging on disaster. What would Rose think of me now, and would she spread the story round the Press Shop? If she did, my humiliation at the hands of Edna and Anna would be mere fleabites compared to the avalanche of derision that would be poured on my cowering head. I could hear them now. 'Who fired off before he even got it out of the holster?' 'Look out fella's, here comes the virgin's delight.' and so on, and so on. Oh yes, I could hear them now alright. Then I remembered that last, soft kiss and knew that my thoughts were unjust. Rose wouldn't spread the story abroad and my failure would remain our secret.

The sound of slow, heavy footsteps approaching my refuge had me shrinking back in the shadows against the door, heart thumping wildly at the thought of – Eric! Could it be that he had followed me for some doting-brother reason? Such as – 'What were ya doin' up the entry whit' me sister, ya dirty little bugger?' Thump! Wallop! Clout! And he could do it too. He was twice – three – four times my size and built like a Centurion Tank into the bargain.

Scarcely daring to breathe, I huddled into the darkest

corner as the shadow lengthened across the doorway – and stopped. A match scraped and flared then the waft of cigarette smoke, mingled with beer fumes, drifted round the corner. I breathed again. If it was Eric, he'd hardly be lighting a fag if he intended to find out just how securely I was held together.

A tuneless humming of *Walking My Baby Back Home* began to float in with the fumes and smoke. I risked a peep outside. A figure was leaning back against the wall, the cigarette dangling from his lips gently bobbing up and down in time to his humming, and he was much too small to be Eric.

He spotted my enquiring head. 'Ello der, our kid' he slurred, sociably. 'Watcharruptoin der den?'

Sheepishly I emerged. 'I'm waiting for the bus.'

He drew extravagantly on his cigarette. 'Das funny – so am I.'

'Oh,' I said, because I couldn't think of anything else to say.

A car drove past, the headlights flashing briefly across us. I had a glimpse of a pale face with a narrow moustache and dark slicked-back hair as my inebriated friend cried : 'Put dat light out! De German bombers is commin!' He cackled, hoisted himself up into a more comfortable position and confided, 'I'm pissed.'

'Oh!' I said, again.

There was a heavy sigh. 'Was you in de war?'

'No. I was only very young, I don't remember much about it.'

He sighed again. 'Bloody awful it was. I lost me mam and dad in dat May blitz, de whole bloody place was on fire.' He shook his fist violently at the sky. 'Bloody Germans! Merderas!'

I wished the bus would hurry up.

He fumbled in his pockets, produced a packet of cigarettes, and asked, 'Ju wanna ciggy?'

'No thanks,' I said. 'I don't smoke.'

He patted me heavily on the shoulder. 'Good lad. An' don't you start, it's bloody awful, smokin.'

'Oh is it?'

He belched loudly and asked, 'An werav you been tonight den?'

'Only to the pictures,' I said.

'Aha!' A finger wagged knowingly. 'I'll bet you was on de back row wit a judy wasn't you, Casanova? Wot's er name den?'

That had me bristling. It was none of his bloody business where I'd been – or who with. 'I went with my mates,' I replied shortly.

The finger wagged accusingly. 'Oh no ya didn't. Youse been wit a judy, I can smell er scent.'

It was a miracle he could smell anything above the stink of beer and smoke.

A bus came rumbling down the hill with the welcome sign Woolton lit up on the front.

'Here's my bus,' I said, hoping to part company with my drunken friend, but it was not to be. Lurching to my side he waved his arm wildly as the bus slowed down and stopped.

There was one chance. Hopping smartly on to the platform, I belted up the stairs. The top deck was almost full, just three seats left, two near the front and one by the stairs. Thankfully I sat down and breathed again.

A loud clatter sounded from below and the sound of an argument floated up the stairs.

'Oh no you don't. I'm not lettin' you up there in that state – you'll break your bloody neck.'

More clattering, and a voice I knew whined, 'Burrive gorra go up der, I wanna a ciggy.'

'Look mate,' said the exasperated conductor, 'you've got two choices. Gerrinside or gerroff, and make your mind up quick 'cos we 'aven't gorrall night!'

A few heavy, unsteady footsteps, the bell rang and I was on my way home.

I met Chris in the bike shed. He galloped over, agog for the lurid details,

He wasn't going to get them.

'Did she turn up?' he asked, eagerly.

'Yes.' I said. 'She did.'

'Well?'

'Well what?'

Even more eagerly. 'Does she wear any?'

'Does she wear any what?'

'Does she wear any knickers you bloody idiot!'

'Yes,' I said. 'She does.'

His face fell slightly. 'Oh. But did you get them off, that's the point?'

'No I didn't. She wouldn't let me near them.'

His mystified look gave me great satisfaction. 'If she wouldn't let you near them, how do you know that she wears any.'

'I asked her.'

Total incredulity. 'You asked her?'

'Yes.' I said, 'All the Toolroom fellas want to know if you wear any knickers? and she said, 'Yes I do.'

'You bloody liar!' he exploded. 'You screwed her didn't you?'

'No I didn't,' I said, loftily. 'She's not like that.'

He laughed derisively. 'Come off it, they're all like that.'

He was still laughing when I delivered the final blow. 'Well big tits isn't for a start, you couldn't get near her!'

Doddy's grinning face greeted me almost before I got through the door. He capered up in his black, shiny boots so full of excitement that he looked as if he were performing some strange, ritualistic clog dance. I could happily have bashed that strawberry nose all over the grinning face but I didn't, because I liked him and I would probably have got the sack.

'How did you get on with that girl?' he cackled.

'You rotten old bugger,' I said. 'What a lousy trick to play. I might have put her in the club.'

And he danced about, roaring with laughter and hugging himself with glee at his cleverness. 'Oh my goodness,' he gasped. 'What a weekend I've had, I never stopped laughing. Every time I thought of you with your trousers round your ankles, trying to roll the finger stall on your plonker I nearly had hysterics. My wife was thinking of having me certified.' And he went off into more paroxysms of laughter.

'I can well imagine,' I said, without enthusiasm. 'But do me a favour, will you Fred?'

'What's that?' he gurgled, wiping his eyes with the back of his hand.

'Don't spread the story around. After that Brylcreem thing my life would be a misery.'

'Fair enough,' he chuckled, 'it's the least I can do after that marvellous weekend. I'll be our secret. Tell me one thing though.'

I knew what was coming but I asked anyway. 'What?'

'Did you get your end away?'

'That's between Rose and me,' I said.

The hooter wailed; machines began humming into life; the Press Shop's rhythmic heartbeat picked up speed. Another week had begun and I was growing up.

Welcome to Meccano Land

The Meccano apprentices with a senior Toolroom member.

A wet lunch hour in the Toolroom. Note the big splodge on the wall from a missile that missed its victim.

The Tool Repair. The author is the guy with the beard.

Frank the Welder with a a home-made spear and wearing a Pig Nosed Bassinett he bought in a junk shop. He was crackers about all things armoured. We became close friends.

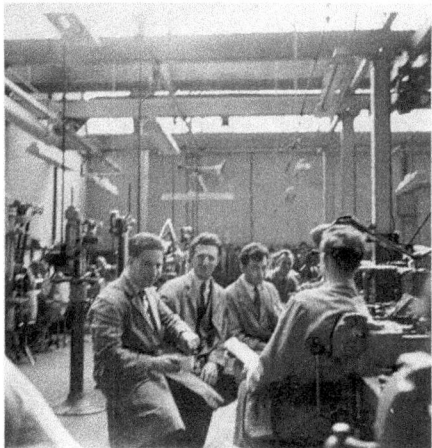

Tea break in the Toolroom.

The Chistmas pantomime actors circa 1950.

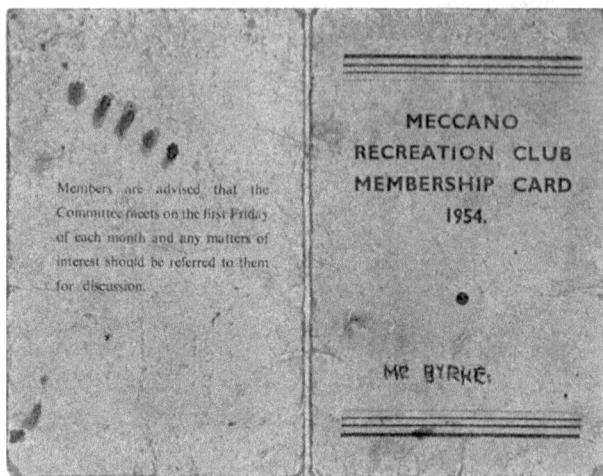

Membership card.

Waitng to clock off time in the Tool Repair. Press Shop opposite.

Budding foremen in the Tool Repairs when the Foreman was at lunch.